Frederick Driscoll

The twelve days' campaign

An impartial account of the final campaign of the late war

Frederick Driscoll

The twelve days' campaign
An impartial account of the final campaign of the late war

ISBN/EAN: 9783742836533

Manufactured in Europe, USA, Canada, Australia, Japa

Cover: Foto ©Andreas Hilbeck / pixelio.de

Manufactured and distributed by brebook publishing software (www.brebook.com)

Frederick Driscoll

The twelve days' campaign

THE

TWELVE DAYS'

CAMPAIGN.

BY

FREDERICK DRISCOLL.

AN

IMPARTIAL ACCOUNT

OF THE

FINAL CAMPAIGN OF THE LATE WAR.

MONTREAL:
PRINTED BY M. LONGMOORE & CO., 67 GREAT ST. JAMES STREET

1866.

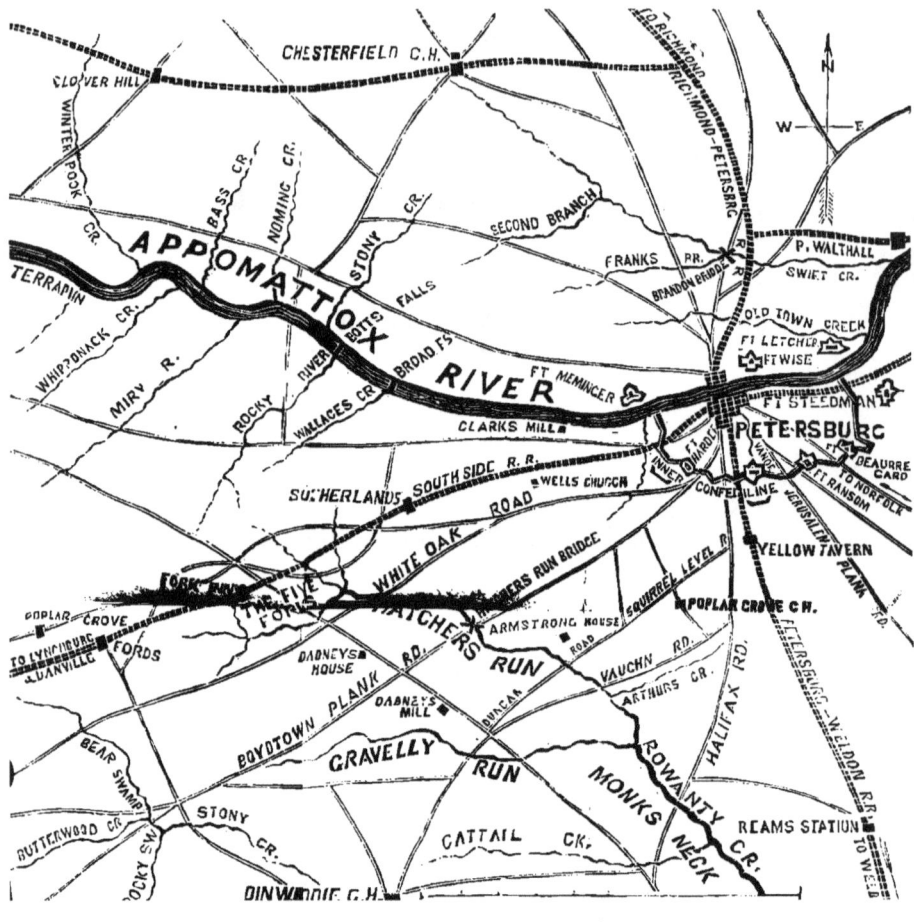

THE
TWELVE DAYS.

On the 29th day of March 1865, began the short campaign that ended in the surrender of the remains of the C. S. Army, under Gen. R. E. Lee. It lasted only *twelve* days, ending on the 9th April.

The forces on each side were very unequal, as there was not less than 90,000 men under the Union flag, against 50,000 of the enemy.

The U. S. army was formed of the 2nd, 5th, 6th, and 9th corps, two divisions of the 24th, and one (colored) of the 25th; in all, 15 divisions, averaging 5,000 men each. This gives a force of 75,000 infantry. Add for one corps of cavalry (three divisions,) 12,000 men, and for artillery, 3,000, and we have a total of 90,000 men. If it was anything less, of those arms, the engineers, &c., would bring it up to that figure.

The C. S. army was formed of the 1st, 2nd, 3rd, and 4th corps, averaging not more than 10,000 men each,* and a small corps of cavalry, numbering about

---

* I was told by a general officer of the enemy, that the 2nd corps had only 4,500 men.

6,000. The artillery, engineers, &c., carried the total force up to some 50,000 men.

As to artillery, there were not less than 200 guns on our side, against 120 or 130 on the other.

The quality of both armies was good, the enemy having the flower of their men who had stood by their tattered battle flags through all vicissitudes; and our army being in most part composed of *aguerri* men, mixed with hardy young recruits.

The condition of the cavalry was unequal, the horses of the enemy being very lean and weak for want of enough food, while those of our cavalry were well fed on short forage,—oats, corn, &c.,—and hay was given them when it could be got.

The disparity in force and in condition led us to look for the great result which was attained.

My despatches and letters will tell the rest.

FIRST DAY,—MARCH 29.

Despatch.

In the Field with the Fifth Corps,
March 29th, 6 P. M.

At 4 A. M. this day, the 2nd and 5th corps were put in march by the Vaughan road upon the right of the enemy's line. On coming to the point where the road crosses the Quaker road, the 2nd division of the 5th corps was left there to hold it, and the other two divisions moved on by the latter road. Passing about one mile and a half beyond Gravelly Run, the head of the column, at 3.30, met a line of the enemy posted on the edge of a thick pine-wood, belting a clearing or farm. Here a sudden and heavy fire was opened upon our skirmish line, and it was driven back upon a line formed of the 1st brigade, 1st division, which, after a sharp fire, forced back the enemy, with some loss in prisoners.

In the meantime General Warren had drawn up the rest of the 1st and 3rd divisions of the 5th corps in line on each side of the road, to support the part engaged.

After an action of about three-quarters of an hour the enemy retreated in haste, leaving his dead and most of his wounded upon the field. The 5th corps now lies upon the ground won.

The force of the enemy engaged to-day was one division of their 4th corps, under Gen. B. Johnson, its strength being about 6,000 men.

Our loss may be 250 to 300 men killed and wounded. That of the enemy seems to be less; but the number of prisoners taken,—some 150—renders their total loss greater than ours.

The place of this day's fight is called Lewis' Farm. The 5th corps was handled by Gen. Warren with his usual ability.

By the movement of to-day, our original line, which extended on the left to Hatcher's Run, has been prolonged beyond the Run to the West, across the Vaughan and Quaker roads, facing north, two and a half miles from Dinwiddie Court House.

SECOND DAY—MARCH 30.

Headquarters Army of the Potomac,
March 30, P. M.

In the face of a heavy rain-storm, which set in last night, and continued until late this afternoon, the army has to-day advanced about two miles, and the Fifth Corps has reached the Boydtown plank-road, near its junction with the White Oak.

This is the place where the Second Corps had an engagement with the enemy last autumn, in which it suffered severely.

The ground gained to-day cost us but few men, the enemy making but very slight resistance.

At Hatcher's Run, which is only a short distance further on, they have strong earthworks erected, defended with heavy guns, and here they will no doubt make a stand to oppose our further advance.

From this point the new line extends east to the Armstrong Mill, the Second Corps holding the right of this position.

Nothing has yet been heard here as to the operations of the Cavalry, but they will, it is not doubted, give a good account of themselves.

A battle is expected to-morrow, for the possession of the South Side Railroad, and judging from the confidence and high spirits of the officers and men, there will be a good result.

THIRD DAY—MARCH 31.

Headquarters Army of the Potomac,
March 31, 1865.

There was severe fighting to-day. In spite of the deep mud the left of our line was pushed forward at daybreak this morning, bringing on a heavy engagement in front of the Fifth Corps and Gen. Miles's division of the Second, the final result of which was the pushing back of the enemy across the White Oak Road, and its occupation by our troops.

At daybreak this morning the 1st Division 5th corps, the left of which rested on the Boydton Road, a short distance above the Quaker Road, moved by the left flank down the Boydton Road to the Butler House, where it was massed behind the commands of Generals Crawford and Ayres, for an advance upon the enemy, covering the White Oak Road.

The object of the advance was the possession of this road, which, diverging from the Boydton Road several miles north of its junction with the Quaker Road, runs westward to the Claiborne Road, leading northwest to the Southside Railroad.

At about 8 o'clock this morning, the Division of Gen. Ayres, supported by those of Crawford and Griffin began their advance upon the enemy, which was immediately resisted by their skirmishers, who were slowly pushed back, however, to within a mile of the White Oak road.

At this moment the enemy, gathering all their available force, and with their usual yell, charged our advancing columns, which, wavering for a time, finally gave way before the impetuous assault, retiring slowly toward the Boydton Plank road, and halting only when they arrived at the brow of a hill, where, supported by Griffin's Division, which had just reached that point, they took shelter in the temporary breastworks constructed by them last night. Several ineffectual attempts were then made by the enemy to dislodge them, our fierce musketry fire, aided by Batteries D and H of the 1st N. Y. Artillery, meanwhile pouring death and destruction into their ranks.

The firing on either side soon subsided into heavy skirmishing, and the rapid interchange of solid shot and shell, lasted until 1 o'clock this afternoon, our troops in the meantime retaining possession of their original line.

At this hour the Division of Gen. Miles, which had been thrown to the left of the Boydton plank-road to close the interval made by the withdrawal of Griffin in the morning, was ordered to strike the enemy in front of the 5th corps on his left flank, while the 5th corps again assayed to obtain possession of the White Oak Road, by advancing simultaneously. The second advance of the corps was led by the 1st Brigade of Griffin's Division, and that of Miles on the right moved in *échelon* in the following order from right to left.

First Brigade, Col. Scott, of the 61st N. Y. commanding; Second Brigade, Col. Nugent, 69th N. Y.; Third Brigade, Gen. Medill; Fourth Brigade, Gen. Ramsay. At 1 o'clock, as before mentioned, the 5th Corps again moved forward upon the enemy, who stubbornly held their ground for some time, when the rapid volleys from the right, and the loud cheer that followed, told of the successful issue of Miles's attack on the enemy's flank as he rolled up their line, now broken, routed, and falling back incontinently, followed by the 5th corps, which was soon in possession of the coveted White Oak Road, which we now retain.

I rode over the battle fields this afternoon, and discovered on every hand traces of a sanguinary conflict. Huge pines were lopped off here and there, and in every direction the trees were splintered and scarred by solid shot, shell, and bullets. The ground was that over which Miles swept down in *échelon* upon the enemy's flank, and the enemy's dead in all positions attested the accuracy of our fire.

While all this was going on, heavy skirmishing was taking place on our line as far as Hatcher's Run. Under cover of a strong skirmish line, Turner's Division, 24th corps, during the afternoon advanced several hundred yards, strongly intrenching, and with its sharp-shooters silenced the guns of several batteries in its front. The first and second brigades of the Third Division of the Second Corps were likewise heavily engaged in skirmishing during the day, and succeeded in assuming an advanced line.

Our casualties will probably reach 1,800 or 2,000,

of which the Fifth Corps is believed to have sustained the loss of nearly one-half.

Among the dead is Major Charles J. Mills, A. A. General to General Humphreys, commanding the Second Corps, who was struck by a round shot and instantly killed, near the junction of the Boydton and Quaker roads.

Major Glenn of the 198th Pa. had the honor of capturing with his own hands, during the engagement of the Fifth Corps to-day, one stand of the enemy's colors, belonging to Horral's brigade of Pickett's Division. General Miles also displayed at his headquarters, this afternoon, a Confederate color taken by his Division.

Gen. Grant was on the line frequently, and during the day moved his headquarters to Danby Mills, near our line of battle.

Reports, apparently well authenticated, come in that Sheridan has this afternoon met with a severe repulse and been forced to fall back through Dinwiddie Court House, leaving many of his wounded in possession of the enemy. Heavy and continuous firing has been heard in that direction this afternoon, and it is not impossible that the cavalry has been repulsed by the enemy.

FOURTH DAY,—APRIL 1.

*Hdqrs. Army of the Potomac, half-a-mile
west of Hatcher's Run,*
April 1st, 1865.

This evening stirring news reached these headquarters from the cavalry under Gen. Sheridan. It stated that he had struck the South Side Railroad, and, in the fight with the enemy taken 4,000 men; also, that the Fifth Corps had taken three batteries. This corps gave full support to the cavalry, and drove back the infantry which enabled the enemy to check Gen. Sheridan in the latter part of yesterday. On receiving this news, Gen. Meade decided to give the enemy no time or chance to send troops to their right, and with this view sent orders to all the Corps—the Second, Twenty-fourth, Sixth and Ninth—to make a simultaneous attack upon the enemy in their front. It was about 9 at night when this order was sent to the corps commanders, and few knew of it. Only the staff were aware that such an order had gone forth, and the men of this great army were going to rest at the time when the fiat of the commanding general was speeding along the long line on its way.

Before turning to this attack, it will be well for me to say what the corps have been doing to-day.

The Second Corps.—All day long this Corps was fighting with the enemy in its front, and gradually fixed its line firmly in spite of their sharp firing. The left of the Corps extended beyond the Boydton road and rested on the White Oak road, there connecting with the Fifth Corps. In front of the Second Corps the enemy had a part of their Third Corps (Hill's), the other part being opposed to the Twenty-fourth Corps, which lies on the right of the Second.

The ground in which the Second Corps was fighting is in most part thick pine woods, and though they afforded very good cover, they were very unfavorable for the action of lines in close order. The ground was, therefore, much in favor of the enemy.

The Twenty-fourth Corps.—This Corps holds the centre of our line, at the point where the Second stood, as stated in my last dispatch. Its left connects with the Second Corps, and rests on Hatcher's Run, while its right touches the left of the Sixth Corps.

At 4 A. M. to-day the enemy made an attack on the Third Brigade with their usual wild yell, in the hope of taking it by surprise. At one point they met with success, driving the 100th N. Y. Volunteers from the line of breast-works, but this did not last long. The 206th Pa. Volunteers, in support, made a charge, forcing them out of the point, and for the rest of the day, the enemy left it alone, though a sharp fire was kept up on both sides. As on the day before, the enemy were unable to work their guns, our sharp-shooters being so close to their batteries, that the gunners dared not expose the least part of their bodies.

The Sixth Corps.—In front of this Corps all was quiet during the day, the enemy being content to hold their lines at that point. On our side the Corps was ready to change this state of rest into one of active attack if it had been advisable, but there was no proof that the enemy had weakened their line at that point, and therefore it was deemed prudent only to observe them closely.

The Ninth Corps.—The same quiet state reigned along the front of this Corps, hardly broken by a few shots from the picket lines; but the Corps was ready to attack, if necessary.

A NIGHT ATTACK.

At 10 o'clock, P.M., a few shots were heard in the front of the Second Corps, and these soon grew into a rattling fire. The enemy at once opened their batteries, and soon the pine woods resounded with the din of a heavy fight.

The firing soon ran along to the front of the Twenty-fourth Corps, and from that to the Sixth, then away to the right, where the Ninth fought. At 11 o'clock the fight was at its acme, and the rattle of musketry was incessant. After two hours' fighting, the sound of the firing in front of the Second Corps began slowly to go back, and a cheer from our line told of some success gained by us.

From that time the firing grew less, and at 2.30 it nearly ceased, leaving us to guess at the new state of things.

This firing arose from an attack made by the enemy.

At 4.30 A. M., just as the grey light began to render things discernible, the firing again broke out in front of the Second Corps, but from a point more to the rear, as if the enemy had taken up a new line. At the same time the sound of a sharp artillery fire came up from the far right, and again the noise of battle shook the pine woods along the front.

At the moment I write (6 A.M.) it is only known that we are gaining ground all along our line.

FIFTH DAY,—APRIL 2.

THE GREAT BATTLE.

Headquarters Army of the Potomac,
April 2, 1865.

To-day I have glad news to communicate. After a series of hard-fought actions this army forced out of their strong lines the enemy who have so long held it at bay. At 4.30 a. m. a general attack was made by all the Corps, which resulted in this great success. The left of our long line, with the cavalry on its flank, turned that of the enemy, who threw back their right from point to point as our army gained ground, and at the end of a glorious day they were found clinging to their last line of defences on their left. I will give a brief report of the action of each Corps in this great operation, as far as it was possible for one person, not gifted with the power of ubiquity, to see, and will begin with

THE SIXTH CORPS.

At 4.30 a. m. this Corps, under Gen. Wright, left its lines to attack that part of the enemy in its front who formed their left centre. The Corps moved in this order: On the right was the First Division, in echelon of brigades, left in front; then came the Second Division, in two lines, and next was the Third, in the same order as the first. This echelon order was used to enable the Corps to throw forward its left and flank the works of the enemy one after another. In a very little time the picket line of the enemy was driven away from its pits, and the line swept on in fine order. Soon a battery of four guns opened upon the First Division, but it did not fire many rounds, for in a rapid charge by the First Brigade it was at once taken, and thus the first work was out of the way.

The batteries of the enemy now opened from every point, and shell flew about the lines, but on they went gallantly. The left soon got near some works in its front, and one by one these fell into our hands. At 10.30 a grand picture of war presented itself. The line of the Corps, with its left in advance, was to be seen sweeping on toward two heavy forts of the enemy, and in rear of its left was the Twenty-fourth Corps coming up in support. At this time the enemy plied their guns vigorously, and shell flew about and burst thickly over our line. The scene was a fine and thrilling one. In the rear, too, was to be seen crowds of men standing upon our earth-works to get a view of the great tableau.

On pushed the left division until it struck the line of the South Side Railroad; and against the two forts swept the Second Division, under Gen. Getty. At the same time the batteries of the latter, posted on rising ground in rear, kept up a sharp fire

B

some rear defences, to which it clung until darkness set in.

The force of the enemy in front of the Fifth Corps was two divisions of their First Corps, together about 7,000 men, which fought under the eyes of Gen. Longstreet.

From these two divisions some 2,000 prisoners were taken in the course of the day—mostly from Picket's Division.

All of the small force of cavalry which the enemy had, also fought on their right, and, with the infantry in support, made a very hard fight of it.

THE SECOND CORPS.

This gallant body, which in every fight has played so high a part, did to the full its share in the battle of to-day, under Gen. Humphrey.

The corps lay on the left of our line, connecting with the right of the fifth, and had some very rough ground to fight upon as well as a brave foe to fight with in the rebel Third Corps (under Gen. Hill). In spite of all, however, it drove the enemy in its front, back, step by step, losing many gallant men in the effort. It may not be too much to say that from 4.30 to-day until dark the Second Corps had very rough work to do, the nature of the ground—thick pine woods—enabling the enemy to fight stubbornly.

In the latter part of the day the enemy was found to have fallen back from this part of the line, owing to the Sixth Corps cutting them off, having reached the South-side Road early in the forenoon, and torn it up. This, of course, cut the Confederate army in two, and the two divisions, thus caught between the Sixth and Second Corps, at once started across the South-side Road toward the Appomattox, hoping to be able to ford it, and thus escape capture. But it appears they ran against Sheridan, and, putting on a bold front, made a show of fight.

News to this effect reaching headquarters, two divisions of the Second Corps were at once sent to flank, and, if possible, capture the entire command.

THE NINTH CORPS.

The line of the enemy's defences in front of this corps was stronger than those at any other point, and consequently the corps had heavy work to do. At the ordered time, 4.30, it made an attack upon the Confederate line of defences stretching to the Appomattox, and carried some of the outer defences. Here the enemy's Second Corps (under General Gordon) fought. It was this body which made the first successful attack upon the line of the Ninth Corps on the 25th ult., and to-day its line was in turn attacked. In the course of the day the Ninth Corps delivered many assaults upon the Confederate lines and met with some successes but lost many men. At the end of the day it found itself close up to the main line of the defences, but unable to go any further.

The first division of the Sixth Corps lent its support to the Ninth Corps, and aided it in the attack.

THE CAVALRY.

This arm was the first to begin the great work of

Corps, who took them by a gallant charge very early in the day. Those were, I think, the first guns taken by the corps, the battery lying first in its way, and not far from the enemy's line of pickets. There were four guns in the battery, and the fourth gun was taken by the 95th Pa., in the same brigade.

Dusk stole over the scene before the force set against the enemy's line at this point was ready, and the attack was deferred for the next day. It was too serious to attack this line of the enemy hastily, for it was their main one. In line the two divisions of the Sixth Corps, the Twenty-fourth Corps, and the Negro Division lay at rest until dark, and then stacked arms, to light fires and cook some food. Tired with the day's fight, the men soon lay down and fell asleep on the field of their glory.

THE TWENTY-FOURTH CORPS

lay in the morning in the new line that it had won the day before in front of our left centre, and at 4:30 a.m. it took its share in the general fight by carrying, with the Second Division, Twenty-fifth Corps, the enemy's works in its front. The corps then moved by its right to lend aid to the Sixth, which had such a heavy task to perform. On coming up, it first lent support to the Sixth corps, and afterward entered into line on its left. The service it did in that position is stated under the action of the Sixth corps, so that I need not go again into an account of it, and space will not allow me to write details.

The action of the Second Division of the Twenty-fifth corps was so connected with that of the Twenty-fourth corps, (with which it acted as if a part of the same corps) that I will not say more of it than what appears in my account of the action of the Sixth.

There is a report that the Twenty-fourth corps lost its leader, Gen. Gibbons, during the day, and I have not heard the report contradicted so far.*

THE FIFTH CORPS.

In the day's great work the part played by this corps was a very high one. On the left of our line, with the cavalry on its left, the Fifth Corps did the great service of turning and driving back the right of the rebel army, formed of their First corps, which was transferred from their left on the 31st ult., as soon as it was seen that our entire force of cavalry was moving round their right.

At 4.30 A.M. the corps made its attack, which was met sharply by the enemy, who, with a weak line, strove by taking advantage of all the cover on the ground to stay the advance. It was all in vain, for the cavalry turned their line at every short stand it made, and the broken sections of it fell back and rallied at some points in the rear, only to be again driven further back.

In this way the right of the enemy was thrown back from point to point, when the Sixth Corps, by the gallant attack referred to, broke through their left centre, and threw their line in fragments back upon

* The report was false.

upon the forts, which did not relax their fire until our men were close up to them. Then a dash was made upon the works, but it was repulsed. Again it was tried, and this time it met with success, but so resolute were some of the enemy inside that they used the bayonet for a short time.

As these two works fell into our hands a loud cheer rent the air, and the enemy were seen hastily retiring to their works next in line, which at once opened sharply in an effort to stay our advance.

SHERIDAN.

About this time Gen. Sheridan came upon the field, and was greeted by a loud cheer from the men of the Sixth Corps, who look up to him with great regard. This must have been a glad moment for him, and the writer never beheld a finer sight, as the Sixth and Twenty-fourth Corps swept on to victory. At this time our entire line was changing its long front to the right, and slowly before it the broken line of the enemy was falling back upon rear defences.

From Battery No. 45 the enemy now fired sharply upon the line of the Second Division, which massed under cover of the two captured works, and got ready for the new task before it. At the same time three batteries were posted at easy range from the enemy's works, and plied them with shell, until they had forced the gunners to leave their guns, and lie under cover of the parapet.

In the meantime the Twenty-fourth Corps came into line on the left of the Sixth, and the First

Division of the latter was sent round to support the Ninth Corps, which had the heaviest part of the great work to do. Against the line of defences that the enemy had fallen back upon, a heavy force was now pitted, and formed in this way: On the left was the Twenty-fourth Corps (two Divisions,) and the Second Division, Sixth Corps; to their right was the Second Division, Twenty-fifth Corps (Colored,) and lastly, on its right, was the third Division of the Sixth Corps. All these, except the Second Division of the Sixth Corps, were fresh troops, and the Negro Division was eager for the fray. As this new line was being formed the enemy shelled it sharply, but the hollows in the ground at that point enabled the dispositions to be made with little loss.

A LULL.

A lull took place when all this force was ready, and it was plain that a distinct action was about to take place. In fact, all the day long the fighting was a series of actions rather than a continuous battle. The enemy had time to gain fresh breath for the coming attack, and looked on quietly at our half-hidden lines reserving their fire for a good mark.

TROPHIES.

Up to this time the trophies gained by us at this point were some 2000 prisoners, four flags, and 25 to 30 guns. Three of the guns were taken by the 65th N. Y., of the First Brigade, First Division, Sixth turning the right of the enemy, and under its dashing leader, Gen. Sheridan, it to-day played a very high part in the battle. The Fifth Corps lent it strong support, and to this body it owes the aid that enabled it to recover from a check and to attack the enemy again under Gen. Fitzhugh Lee, with most of their First Corps in support of him. From the latter was taken in the fight on the 1st the 1,000 men of Picket's Division.

It was thought to-day that our cavalry had got round upon the enemy's line of retreat upon Lynchburg.

THE ENEMY'S LINE

Was formed of four corps in this order. On their right with the cavalry on the flank, was the First Corps. Next to it was the Fourth Corps, then the Third, and lastly, with its left resting upon the Appomattox, the Second Corps.

There were Fitz Lee, Longstreet, Hill, Gordon and Anderson, and under them were such men as Heth, Wilcox, Picket, Kershaw, Field, Ransom and others.

GENERAL LEE.

Coolly directing the battle in this crisis was Gen. Lee, who, it must be said, made a hard fight of it, and showed his usual ability. He fought against numbers and made the best of it. His total force did not exceed 50,000 men of all arms, and it fought on a line 23 miles in extent. It is to be inferred from the strategy of Gen. Lee, that he fought under orders to hold his lines till the last. If he had left Richmond to its fate, ten or twelve days sooner, he could have carried off his army with small loss, and, by forced marches, have effected a junction with Gen. Johnson.

OUR LOSSES.

It is not easy to guess at our losses to-day. I think that 6,000 men in all will cover it. The Ninth Corps lost most, and next to it the Second. The loss is not at all equal to the great results gained.

PRISONERS.

During the day I saw some 2,000 prisoners taken about the centre of our line; and I think the total number taken to-day may reach 4,000 to 6,000 men.

MEN OF NOTE LOST.

I have heard only of the name of Gen. Gibbon as on the list of killed. Of men of lesser note there was Gen. Grant, in command of a brigade of the first division Sixth Corps; and Cols. Crosby, 61st Pa., and Holt, 49th N.Y., (both dead,) of the first division Sixth Corps.

To-morrow great results are looked for.

cess. Apple-jack is a pleasant drink for any one who drinks, and in an army who does not drink?

At most of the stores or better houses there were guards placed by order of the Provost-Marshal. Any citizen who applied for guard against pillage, got it. The number of men thus on duty was very large to-day.

RAILROAD TO CITY POINT.

The road to City Point is being put in running order in the least possible time, and it will be open for traffic by to-morrow. Supplies can then be brought direct to the city, which will serve as a base for a time. Light boats will soon be able to run up the Appomattox, so that plenty will soon reign where want has been so much felt.

Young men are to be seen in the streets of an age fit for service, and this surprised the writer not a little considering the rigid conscription of the Confederate Government. By some means or other, many of the young men of this city have managed to evade the law.

THE WOMEN

seem to have fared better than the men, for few of them showed any signs of want, and many of the young women of this city are very well looking, but they affect to avert their looks from any one in a blue coat; evidently the men in grey have been in favor with them.

PRESIDENT LINCOLN

was here this day for a time, and no doubt was well pleased to see the inside of a city which has so long held out against our army. For a few days he has been staying at City Point in expectation of the event which has now been realized.

THE CAMPAIGN.

On the 31st ultimo, the third day after the campaign opened, there seemed reason to doubt that the success which has attended our army was going to be met with, but all has so far ended well.

OUR LOSSES.

Of course no reports of our losses can yet be got. All are too busy with the enemy now to attend to lists of casualties, and it is as much as can be done to take care of the wounded.

THE ENEMY

commenced evacuating last night at 10 o'clock, and by three o'clock this morning were across the river, having burned about a million dollars' worth of tobacco, the Southside Railroad depot and the bridges across the Appomattox.

The Mayor of the town met the troops as they entered, and handed to the officer commanding the and the tram bridge over the Appomattox was reduced to a few charred beams. These fires were the work of the enemy, who were resolved to leave nothing of use to us behind.

A WELCOME.

At first when our troops entered the city most of the women were to be seen waving something or other white, in token of welcome and peace. On the faces of some were real smiles, and on those of others the smile no doubt dissembled a bitter heart, fear more than anything else led the Southern fair sex to greet the army with this mockery of a welcome.

THE NEGROES.

They showed signs of real gladness at our coming, and this was the more evinced by the old men who sang as we passed them; and some even, in the warmth of their delight, took hold of the hands of our men and sang a welcome with a few capers by way of keeping time to the chant. At this the boys would burst into loud laughs which the old negroes would take for plaudits, and go away singing the louder.

THE MARKETS.

In my peregrinations I went by some markets—empty markets; nothing was there for sale—no meat, no vegetables, nor anything else. It is true when I passed by the markets it was not the time for business, but there was a very evident lack of the necessaries of life.

FOOD

Was so scarce that the poor went out to our old camps to pick up the rations of beef and hard bread lying about there, and many carried off the blankets they found lying in the log huts. The contrast between plenty on our side and want on the other was very great. There was a total lack of business in the city, and the writer only wondered how the people managed to live. All wore a thin, sallow look of want, that it was sad to see.

TOBACCO.

Of this there seemed to be any quantity. Indeed the great features were a want of food and an abundance of tobacco. Our men were to be seen going about with large bunches stuck in their belts or in their hands. There seemed to be a glut of the weed, and in wanton play the men threw bunches at each other.

"APPLE-JACK."

This, too, was found to be plenty by those who were cunning in the bringing to light of such things, and many a fellow was to be seen reeling about under its potent influence; but I saw no cases of great ex-

SIXTH DAY—APRIL 3.

Headquarters Army of the Potomac,
April 3, 1865.

CAPTURE OF GUNS.

The results of the battle are as great as I was led to expect. The entire line of the enemy's defences fell into our hands at 5 a. m. to-day. At least 38 guns were taken in the fight, 16 being captured by the Sixth Corps, and the rest in most part by our cavalry. The guns taken by the Sixth Corps have been sent to City Point; they were mostly twelve-pound—some being steel and the rest brass. But the best result was the forcing of the great Confederate army into the field, where it cannot make any stand against our numerous army, flushed with success.

ENTRY INTO PETERSBURG.

The General-Commanding and staff passed through the city at 11 a.m., this day, and took the field by the Appomattox. In order to get a good view of the battle field from the enemy's side, I went out on the Weldon Road as far as Battery 40. This work covers the railroad and the lead works by the side of it.

The latter have not been used for a long time, I learn.

THE WORKS.

Battery 40, and the line of defences to its right and left, including Battery 45, were still held by the enemy when night put an end to the battle of yesterday and these they evacuated in the dead of night.

This section of the line was not really so strong as it appeared to be from our line, and it could have been carried. In rear of Battery 40 was another line of defences covering the South Side Railroad, and the fire of these could command the works in its front; this also could have been taken, but it would have cost us a serious loss of life, which was spared by allowing the enemy time to quit the works.

THE CITY.

On passing through the city I saw most of the stores closed, and few people in the streets; the Ninth Corps was the first to enter, and some of its flags were hoisted upon the Court-House.

FIRES.

Some large fires were to be seen in the street—one of a large tobacco warehouse near the Jarret House and the air was filled with the fumes of tobacco.

The depot of the Norfolk Railroad was also on fire,

following communication, offering the surrender of the city :

Lieutenant-General U. S. Grant, Commanding Armies of the U. S., or the Major-General commanding United States forces in front of Petersburg :

GENERAL : The City of Petersburg having been evacuated by the Confederate troops, we, a committee authorized by the Common Council, do hereby surrender the city to the United States forces, with a request for the protection of the persons and property of its inhabitants.

We are, respectfully, your obedient servants,

W. W. TOWNES, Mayor,
D'ARCY PAUL, Committee.

Petersburg, April 3, 1865.

RICHMOND.

DETAILS OF THE OCCUPATION.

Ballard House, Richmond,
April 3, 1865.

Ere this you will have become aware of the fact that Richmond has fallen. It was surrendered to our troops by the Mayor of the city at 8 a.m. this day. The second brigade of the third division Twenty-Fourth Corps, commanded by Gen. Ripley, led the advance upon the town, Gen. Weitzel and his staff at the head of the column.

ENTERING THE CITY.

Upon entering the suburbs of the city, General Weitzel sent a small detachment of the 4th Mass. cavalry, under the command of Major Stevens, to meet the Mayor of the city, from whom the general received the keys of the public buildings. The Army of the James then marched triumphantly into the rebel capital, having met with no opposition whatever.

After leaving our works in front of the enemy's intrenchments, our army was greeted with cheers by the populace, who have thus far behaved in a becoming manner, and have shown us every respect.

THE NEGROES.

The negroes were excessively jubilant and danced for very joy at the sight of their sable brethren in arms, the Twenty-Fifth Corps, who followed close upon the heels of Gen. Ripley's brigade of the twenty-fourth corps, in the entry of the Union forces into Richmond.

About daylight on the morning of the surrender,

our forces were formed in line in front of our works before the city, and were then moved up by Gen. Weitzel. A few stray shots were fired by the retreating enemy, hitting no one. Beyond this no opposition was offered us and our troops filed into the enemy's works and up the Osborne and Newmarket road to the city.

A look into the enemy's works disclosed the fact of their having left in great haste. Many of their quarters were left without a thing being taken out of them. Pistols, revolvers, carbines and arms of every description were found in profusion, clothing of every description was in abundance, and in some of the officers' quarters were found their private correspondence, diaries, &c.

While stragglers were pillaging the deserted camps our army continued its march toward the city. The enemy had planted torpedoes in front of Fort Gilmore, and so thickly, that it was found necessary to march the column in single file through the fort. They had attached to every torpedo a stick with a piece of red webbing tied to it, to mark the locality of the infernal machines. This precaution they had observed for the safety of their own men. General Weitzel had some days previously been informed of the fact of their having planted the torpedoes and how they were marked.

The General's precaution of not moving until daylight over the ground immediately in front of Fort Gilmore was a very wise one, as, had the torpedoes been exploded, the destruction of life must necessarily have been great.

IN RICHMOND.

A couple of hours more brought us into the heart of the enemy's capital.

The sight of the burning buildings was truly sorrowful. That part of the city along the river front known as the main business part was one vast sheet of flame.

What with the roaring of the flames, and the burning and tumbling buildings, the shouts of our soldiers moving up the main streets to the Capitol, the music of our bands playing favorite airs, the shouts of welcome and the excitement of the people, there was a scene of grandeur and magnificence never to be effaced from memory.

The thought of entering Richmond, that city which was the objective point of a four years' war in such a style without a struggle, after many hard fought battles to possess it, in which thousands of our brave men have been slain, was calculated to thrill the hearts of all in the column.

General Weitzel immediately established his headquarters in the State Capitol, in the hall lately occupied by the Virginia House of Delegates, and immediately instituted measures to restore order to the town, as all was a Babel of confusion.

The following order was issued by General Weitzel, directly after taking up his headquarters in the city :

Hdqrs. Detachment Army of the James,
Richmond, Va., April 3, 1865.

Major-General Weitzel, commanding detachment

of the Army of the James, announces the occupation of the City of Richmond by the armies of the United States under command of Lieut.-Gen. Grant. The people of Richmond are assured that we come to restore to them the blessings of peace, prosperity and freedom, under the flag of the Union. The citizens of Richmond are requested to remain for the present quietly within their houses, and to avoid all public assemblages or meetings in the public streets. An efficient Provost guard will immediately reestablish order and tranquillity within the city. Martial law is for the present proclaimed. Brig.-Gen. George F. Shepley, United States Volunteers, is hereby appointed Military Governor of Richmond. Lieut.-Col. Fred. S. Manning, Provost-Marshal-General of the Army of the James, will act as Provost-Marshal of Richmond. Commanders of detachments doing guard duty in the city will report to him for instructions.

By command of Maj.-Gen. Weitzel,

D. D. WHEELER, A. A. G.

THE ENEMY'S REAR GUARD.

The rear guard, a small body of cavalry, retreated in the direction of Lynchburg, only a few minutes before our advance entered the town. The main body of the enemy commenced to retreat about 10 o'clock the preceding Sunday evening. Their destination was believed to have been Lynchburg, but whether they will strike for that point, when they come to learn the strait which Lee, with the main body of his army, has been forced into is doubtful.

JEFF. DAVIS.

Jefferson Davis remained in the city till dark Sunday night, having, however, sent his family to Charlotte, N. C., some time during the preceding week.

The inhabitants generally were not informed of the contemplated evacuation until they saw the Confederate troops passing through the town from the east. Then the truth flashed upon them that they were to be left to the mercy of the Yankees.

A number of these, fearful that their past misdeeds would not recommend them to the clemency of the United States Government, hastily left their all to share the fate and fortunes of the C. S. army, an army so shattered that it can hardly be dignified by that name.

DAMAGE BY THE FIRE.

The damage done by the fire was very great. The finest portions of Main Street and the street below, fronting the river, have been laid waste by the devouring element.

The Libby Prison still stands, surrounded on all sides by a heap of smoking and burning ruins. Within its loathsome walls are now confined what rebel soldiers were secured in the capture of Richmond.

ORIGIN OF THE FIRE.

I am informed that the conflagration was occasioned by the enemy firing a number of the Confederate storehouses, containing tobacco and other stores, which they were unable to remove before the evacuation of the city, owing to the confusion existing in all quarters.

No trustworthy estimate can be formed of the amount of property destroyed. The Court-House and all the bridges over the James River leading into Manchester were burnt.

The *Dispatch* and *Examiner* newspaper offices are also in ruins, and the streets in the vicinity of the fire are littered with the debris of household furniture, &c.

Private and public papers and documents are scattered over the street, subject to the winds and the rapacity of the piccaninnies who in innumerable swarms—in danger of falling walls—were diving with their little black hands into every place that suggested a reward for their pains.

The colored people were extremely enthusiastic over our arrival and greeted us with the heartiest welcome in a characteristic manner, and "De Lord bress the Yankees" was heard on every side.

THE WHITES.

The whites thus far have treated us with great cordiality, and on our first entry into the city cheered us vociferously. A few of the loud mouthed and hasty "Rebs" got themselves into trouble by a too free use of their tongues, and they speedily found themselves confined to close quarters in a room in the building occupied by the Provost-Marshal.

Gen. Weitzel has taken for his private residence the mansion of Mr. Davis. A portion of his staff are quartered with him, and the remainder in a splendid dwelling a few doors below.

The interior of Davis's house presented the appearance of having been very hastily evacuated by him. Everything is in fine order and in good repair. Many of Mrs. Davis's little nicknacks and ornaments are yet to be found on the mantles and bureaus of her room.

THE FORTIFICATIONS.

The cordon of works around the city I have as yet had little time to examine. A glance at them, however, satisfies me that their strength has in no wise been exaggerated. The forts are mostly of a massive size, and are situated in naturally impregnable positions, well mounted with guns of the heaviest calibre.

The number of guns captured in the works around the city is roughly estimated at about three hundred. They were all spiked, but otherwise left uninjured.

The powder magazine in Fort Darling, and the enemy's rams in the James River below, were blown up with a terrific noise. The shock was distinctly felt for miles around.

All the steamers at the wharves—with the exception of the William Allison, flag-of-truce steamer—were destroyed, together with a new ironclad upon the stocks.

The yard around the State Capitol is literally covered with the household utensils of the burned-out families. The Capitol itself has not been injured.

The residents here firmly believe that the Rebellion has received its death-blow, and are rejoicing over their release from the rule of Jefferson Davis.

Our soldiers have conducted themselves in a becoming manner, much to the astonishment of the people, who expected that vengeance would be visited upon them.

SEVENTH DAY—APRIL 4.

*Headquarters Army of the Potomac,
in the Field,* April 4, 1865.

RACE FOR DANVILLE.

This day was spent by the army in an active pursuit of the enemy. It is a foot-race again between the two great bodies for a certain goal. The point for which General Lee is thought to be in march is Danville. Under cover of his left he drew off from his lines on the night of the 2nd, and began a rapid march in the hope of gaining a good start upon us, in which he has failed, for this army is well up with his rear guard, the Second Corps, under General Gordon, which held the left of his lines on the day of the great battle.

By the Cox Road the bulk of this army marched on Monday, through Petersburg, in pursuit, and the cavalry has been on the heels of the enemy all this day, taking 2,000 more men from their ranks, which are fast dwindling away. It is thought that there cannot be more than 35,000 men now with Gen. Lee, and as they go on the men quit the ranks and find their way home.

OUR CAVALRY

gives no rest to the broken enemy, and is pressing hard upon the rear of Gordon's Corps (their 2nd). It is from it that most of the prisoners are taken by our cavalry. In many of the houses along the line of march, parties of wounded men are found, who, having been able to march from the late field of battle, were taken along, and had to fall out on the way. It is only a very sanguine Confederate who cannot see that all is lost with the lately great army of Northern Virginia.

ITS DAYS ARE NUMBERED.

It may not exist as an organized body thirty days longer. If it can reach the force under Gen. Joseph Johnson, a second heavy fight will take place, this time with Gen. Sherman; but the Army of the Potomac would in less than ten hours enter into the fight, and the result to the enemy's forces would be a disaster which would be final.

The 1st of May may see the end of this war, for nothing but a heavy line of defences could enable the enemy to make a stand again, and time to throw up such a line is now wanting. The enemy can only flee from point to point for a short time.

HILL'S LOSS

to the enemy is great, for he led their Third Corps with ability, and was perhaps only second to General

Lee in importance to the Confederate army. In the late fight his corps was almost ubiquitous. It extended from Hatcher's Run to Battery Gregg, and fought our Twenty-fourth and Sixth Corps. It was in that work that Hill was struck by three balls, which made his death wounds.

OUR ADVANCE.

To-day the cavalry and the leading corps made a long march. The Ninth Corps is some distance in the rear, as it left Petersburg only to-day, but the rest of the army is well in hand, and the cavalry, under the untiring Sheridan, is doing great service.

There are many reports of extravagant success on our part, flying about. One is that 20,000 of the enemy have been forced to lay down their arms, but this is at least premature. It is the old story of bagging. The army is doing well, but has not made such short work of the enemy as that.

BURKESVILLE

may be the point at which another great fight will take place. It is sixty miles from Petersburg, and the army has not made more than about half that distance up to this evening.

My next dispatch will likely carry the news of another heavy blow inflicted upon the enemy.

EIGHTH DAY—APRIL 5.

This day also was spent in pursuit. By forced marches all the corps pushed on, flushed with success, while the cavalry were far in the advance, essaying to head off the enemy from their line of retreat.

The latter were hurrying off as fast as their legs could carry them, but showed fight to our cavalry when pushed too closely. They were the flower of the enemy, who would fight to the last; and their spirit was not broken. So hard run were they, however, that, I was told by the negroes, they went into the fields and even sucked the teats of the cows, having very little time to milk them, and being too weak to wait for the usual way of getting the milk.

Burkesville was the point for which all our columns were in march, it being the point where the Danville Railroad is intersected by the South-side road.

The enemy threw up some sort of a breast-work every night to strengthen his lines. These were generally shallow rifle pits with fence-rails piled on the top of the earth, the trench being very bare cover for a line of men kneeling.

It was to me a matter for wonder how men so hard run could hold together and make any fight of it. It was spirit more than discipline, which enabled them to do so, for the latter was gone. The men only carried their arms, a blanket, and a havresack if they had one, so that they were in light marching order, and could keep ahead of ours.

NINTH DAY—APRIL 6.

Headquarters 6th Corps,
April 6.

To-day the 6th Corps moved to Jettersville by the shortest practicable road to the left of Deatonville, with the object of taking position on the left of the Second Corps, striking the road running from Deatonville to Burke's Station at a point a little to the southward of the former place. It was found that the Second Corps was engaged at the front and right, and the cavalry, heavily, to the left. Moving down the road toward Burke's Station, perhaps a mile, and turning sharp to the right, the 6th Corps proceeded across toward a nearly parallel road, on which the enemy was moving, and along which he had thrown up a line of intrenchments.

As soon as the leading Division (Gen. Seymour's) could be formed it was moved up on the road held by the enemy, which was carried. Then turning to the left, it was advanced down the road against a pretty strong resistance. By this time the 1st Division was put in position, as rapidly as possible, on Seymour's left.

The lines were again advanced, and we swept down the road for a distance of about two miles. Arriving at a deep and difficult creek we found the enemy had reformed his line on the opposite side, where we attacked and drove him to a point, a distance of half a mile further.

In the first attack a portion of the cavalry operated on our right flank. In its subsequent attack the mass of cavalry operated on our right and left flank of the enemy.

The result had been a complete success. The combined forces captured five General officers, among them Gens. Ewell, and Custis Lee, and large numbers of other prisoners.

The 6th Corps go in camp about two miles beyond this point and await instructions. The First and Third Divisions and the artillery engaged to-day, behaved admirably. The casualties were not very considerable.

The Corps has nobly sustained the reputation it earned on the 2nd inst., as well as upon its many previous hard fought battle fields.

The following despatch from Army Head Quarters will explain what was done with the 2nd and 5th Corps on this date :

Lieut.-Gen. GRANT :—At daylight this morning, I moved the Second, Fifth and Sixth Army Corps along the railroad in the direction of Amelia Court House. Soon after moving trustworthy intelligence was received that the enemy was moving toward Farmville.

The direction of the Second and Fifth Army Corps was immediately changed from a northerly to a northwesterly direction, and the directing Corps, the Second, moving on Deatonville, and the Fifth, heretofore in the centre, moved on the right of the Second, and the Sixth, facing about and moving by the left flank, taking position on the left of the Second. It was understood the cavalry would operate on the extreme left.

The changes were promptly made, the Second Army Corps soon becoming engaged with the enemy near Deatonville, drawing him by his right across Sailor's Creek to the Appomattox. The Fifth Army Corps made a long march, but its position prevented its striking the enemy's column before it had passed. The Sixth Army Corps came up with the enemy about four p.m., and, in conjunction with the Second Corps on its right and cavalry on its left, attacked and routed the enemy, capturing many prisoners, among them Lieutenant-General Ewell and General Custis Lee.

I transmit dispatches both from Gens. Humphreys and Wright, which, in justice to these distinguished officers and the gallant corps they command, I beg may be sent to the War Department for immediate publication. It is impossible at this moment to give any estimate of casualties on either side, or of the number of prisoners taken, but it is evident to-day's work is going to be one of the most important of the recent brilliant operations.

The pursuit will be continued as soon as the men have a little rest.

Griffin, with the Fifth Army Corps, will be moved by the left, and Wright and Humphreys continue the direct pursuit as long as it promises success.

GEORGE G. MEADE, Major-Gen.

TENTH DAY—APRIL 7.

In the Field with the Sixth Corps, near Farmville, April 7, 1865.

To-day the army reached the Appomattox at this point, and after a trifling resistance, passed the stream.

THE APPOMATTOX

here is a mere shallow creek running over a sandy bed. Three bridges spanned it, one being the railroad bridge, a second the Cumberland, and the third the Buffalo. All these were destroyed by the enemy after they had crossed. They passed at 8 a. m. with a long waggon train. On our coming in sight of the Appomattox, we found the railroad bridge on fire and the other two destroyed.

A short pontoon bridge was laid, and the Second Corps soon passed the stream, covered by a strong skirmish line. Very little artillery was used, not more than twenty shots being fired.

THE GROUND

about the Appomattox here is hilly, and offered good

positions for our batteries, which could have swept the other bank of the stream if the enemy had made a stand there.

Farmville is a small town, divided by the Appomattox, and has perhaps 2,000 inhabitants. Its site is a rather picturesque one, on the slopes of the little stream. It has a thriving look, but was found by our foragers to be very poor in food. The people took their change of situation very quietly, and, for the most part, stayed in-doors. The place is about 50 miles from Lynchburg.

THE CONFEDERATE ARMY

is said by the people to be very much reduced—not to number half of ours. It cannot have more than 35,000 men left, and in guns it must be very deficient. By the heavy "bag" made by us yesterday—the first really large body of prisoners taken by us at one time —Gen. Lee has also lost some of his best Generals, Ewell being one of them.

OUR ADVANCE

has been rapid, and has given no time to the enemy to recover from the heavy blows dealt at him. The cavalry and Second and Fifth Corps lie on the other side of the Appomattox, while the Sixth is in bivouac on the hills this side (east) of the stream. The Ninth and Twenty-fourth Corps, and a Division (the Second) of the Twenty-fifth are in rear. The army is well in hand, and in fine spirits.

The roads are much broken about a mile back from the Appomattox, and the rain to-day rendered them nearly impassable; but the weather so far has favored us. To-day the scene along the line of march was the same old Virginia one of rain, mud, and a long line of waggons splashing through a broken road, drawn by mules covered with mud from hoofs to tip of ear.

THE COUNTRY.

The line of march to-day was through a hilly but fresh country, many of the farms being in a state of good cultivation, and small stacks of corn were found on most of them, though the half of last year's crops had been taken by the Government as a tax. In most of the houses the women remained and some of the old men. As to the young men they were "in the army," that is in the Rebel army. Very little live stock was to be seen, and the lowing of a cow made our foragers prick up their ears, so to speak.

THE VENABLE HOUSE.

On the east side of the Appomattox, about half a mile from this point, and on a fine plantation of ground, is the Venable House. There Gen. Joseph E. Johnson was born, and the family has given several men to the Confederate army, one of whom is Major Venable, on Gen. Lee's staff. The house was an object of interest to us as we passed.

SHERIDAN

is far in the front, sweeping on with untiring vigour, the Murat of our army. His cavalry pick up prisoners in parties. In the course of the day some 500 prisoners were taken, many of whom were very glad to get out of their bondage.

PILLAGE AND THROAT-CUTTING.

There has been a good deal of pillage done by our men, and the consequence is that some of them have been found shot, or throat cut, in the woods. This is the fate of pillagers in the country of an excited enemy. The Provost-Marshals did much to put a stop to marauding. I saw two of them drub with the flat of their sabres a squad of these fellows, who ran off as fast as their legs could carry them.

The enemy have only six hours' start of us, and are not gaining in this grand foot race.

I am sorry to say that Gen. J. A. Smith, in command of the Third Brigade, Second Division, Second Corps, was killed in to-day's fight. His loss is much regretted by us all.

ELEVENTH DAY—APRIL 8.

In the Field with the Sixth Corps,
April 8, 1865.

To-day the Army left the Appomattox, moving in three columns by as many roads which converge at Appomattox Court-House, on the way to Lynchburg.

The cavalry and Fifth Corps took a road to the left of the old stage road. The Twenty-fourth Corps went by another road to the right of them, and the Second and Sixth Corps took the old stage road. This was the one followed by the enemy.

The plan of movement is for the cavalry and Fifth and Twenty-fourth Corps to head off the enemy from any route to Danville, which General Lee still seems to seek, and to force him to go toward Lynchburg, which is reported to be now in the hands of General Stoneman.

The action about the Appomattox yesterday was more serious than I was led to suppose. The First Brigade of the First Division, Second Corps, commanded by Colonel G. W. Scott, lost heavily, and this gallant officer was himself struck by a spent ball.

During this day the Sixth Corps met with no enemy, and the Second Corps was equally free in its march. The two Corps marched about 16 miles over a good road.

The line of march passed through a finer and fresher country than any part we have seen yet. As we go west the farms appear better cultivated, and less devoid of stock. There was the same pillage to be seen to-day as on the march to the Appomattox, and the number of stragglers was shameful. They showed an utter disregard for discipline; yet there was no excuse for all this marauding, for the men had drawn three days' rations.

To-night I learn that the cavalry have taken fourteen more guns and 1,200 to 1,500 prisoners. This loss must leave Gen. Lee with less than 30,000 men, and very little artillery. A few more days of such work, and the enemy will be undone.

To-morrow the Sixth Corps will effect a junction with the Second, and the two will move on together toward Lynchburg, on the heels of the enemy, while the cavalry and Fifth and Twenty-Fourth Corps, moving by a road to the left, will turn them from any route that leads to Danville.

In the Field with the Sixth Corps,
Beyond the Appomattox, April 8—10 a.m.

A report has just come to me that General Lee has sent in a member of his staff to ask what terms would be granted him if he surrendered the remains of his army.

General Ewell, who is in our hands, is said to have mentioned that his Chief would do this.

More than the report I cannot learn at this hour, and must send it meagre as it is, my messenger being about to go.

TWELFTH AND LAST DAY—APRIL 9.

Headquarters Army of the Potomac, 4 miles east of Appomattox Court House, April 9, 1865.

The wires will have carried you the glad news of this day before my dispatch can reach you. I will, therefore, only give the news more in detail.

MOVEMENTS.

After a march of about 12 miles, the column of the army moving by the old stage road to Lynchburg, came to this point. The Second and Sixth Corps formed the column, and the Second was in front, with its First Division leading. At this point a flag of truce was seen in front of the skirmish line, and Gen. Miles, in command of the division, sent one of his staff, Capt. J. D. Cook, A. D. C., to meet it. On going out, this officer found Col. Taylor, Gen. Lee's Chief of Staff, with a written communication for Gen. Meade. Capt. Cook took in the note, which made a request that this army would suspend hostilities until Gen. Lee could fully consider the terms offered him yesterday by Gen. Grant. To this the Commanding General replied, that he was not authorized to grant a suspension of hostilities, but that he would give two hours for Gen. Lee to accede to the terms, and if at the end of that time he did not do so, this army would continue its advance. The two hours were passed by us in agreeable suspense. At the end of that time the order was given to advance, and the Second Corps was hardly ten minutes in motion when a staff officer of the enemy came in with a note from Gen. Grant, sent on by Gen. Lee, directing the Commanding General of this army to suspend hostilities until further orders, and adding that General Grant would be with him in half an hour. On receipt of this, Gen. Meade gave the necessary order, and the army came to a halt.

At 2.30 p. m., Gen. Grant arrived and held a conference with Gen. Lee, the result of which was that the latter agreed to surrender the remainder of his army, now reduced to about 20,000 men, as prisoners-of-war, to be paroled and sent home, not to serve until duly exchanged, and is to sign articles to that effect.

DARING RESOLUTION.

From the staff officer who came in we learn that Gen. Lee ordered all his trains and the carriages of such guns as he did not intend to use—everything, in fact, that could not be carried on horseback—to be burned last night, in order that the enemy might be free to cut his way through our cavalry. This he tried to do to-day, but met the Twenty-Fourth Corps, which was with the cavalry, on a road to our left. Finding himself thus met, Gen. Lee abandoned his intention, which might have been successful if there had been only cavalry to fight at the point where he expected to find only cavalry.

GENERAL LEE.

Col. Taylor, the Chief of Staff of Gen. Lee, in chatting with Captain Cook, said that the General, though calm, was in depressed spirits at the straits to which he saw his army reduced; and that for the two last days he was in rear of his main column, not more than ten minutes ride from our advance, so closely did he watch the movements of this army.

The officers and men of the Confederate army were anxious to hear what was to be done with Gen. Lee, and showed great concern for him, saying that they did not care for themselves, but only for "the old man."

VIEW OF OUR OPERATIONS.

There can be only one view of our operations, and it is that they have been short, sharp and decisive. They have been a fine combination against the enemy which has been well executed. To our strong force of cavalry and the untiring activity of Gen. Sheridan may be ascribed the decisive success that our arms have met with; but it must be added that the action of the Sixth Corps, on the second instant, and on the 6th, and the support of the Second, Fifth and Twenty-fourth Corps, have contributed greatly to the results. All our corps commanders have done well, but Gens. Sheridan and Wright have, owing to circumstances, been able to strike more vital blows at the enemy than those of the other officers.

In twelve short days these great results have been gained. Who would have thought it? From our great numerical superiority, I had an idea the campaign would be over in 30 days, and, in one of my letters, mentioned the 1st of May as the time it would likely come to an end; but the time has been even shorter.

THE ARTICLES OF SURRENDER.

A copy of these is not to be had at headquarters to-night, but one will no doubt be officially published to-morrow.

A copy of the notes interchanged between the two commanding generals, in regard to the surrender of the C. S. Army, will be found below.

On the 7th Gen. Lee was asked to surrender the remains of his army, to which he answered:

April 7, 1865.

GENERAL,

I have received your note of this day.

Though not entirely of the opinion you express of the hopelessness of further resistance on the part of the Army of Northern Virginia, I reciprocate your desire to avoid the useless effusion of blood, and, therefore, before considering your proposition, ask the terms you will offer on condition of its surrender.

R. E. LEE,
General.

LT.-GEN. U. S. GRANT,
    Commanding Army of the
        United States.

April 8, 1865.

GEN. R. E. LEE,
    Com'dng C. S. A.,

GENERAL,

Your note of last evening in reply to mine of same date, asking the conditions on which I will accept the surrender of the Army of Northern Virginia, is just received.

In reply I would say that, peace being my first desire, there is but one condition I insist upon, viz.:

That the men surrendered shall be disqualified for taking up arms against the Government of the United States, until properly exchanged.

I will meet you, or designate officers to meet any officers you may name for the same purpose, at any point agreeable to you, for the purpose of arranging definitely the terms upon which the surrender of the Army of Northern Virginia will be received.

   Your ob'dnt Servant,
    U. S. GRANT,
     Lt. General,
    Commanding Armies of the
     United States.

April 8, 1865.

GENERAL,

I received, at a late hour, your note of to-day, in answer to mine of yesterday.

I did not intend to propose the surrender of the Army of Northern Virginia, but to ask the terms of your proposition. To be frank, I do not think the emergency has arisen to call for the surrender; but, as the restoration of peace should be the sole object of all, I desire to know if your proposals tend to that end.

I can not, therefore, meet you with a view to surrender the Army of Northern Virginia; but, so far as your proposition may affect the C. S. forces under my command, and tend to peace, I should be pleased to meet you at 10 a.m. to-morrow, on the old Stage Road to Richmond, between the picket lines of the two armies.

Your obd'nt Servant,
R. E. LEE, General,
Commanding C. S. Army.

LT.-GEN. U. S. GRANT,
　Commanding U. S. Armies.

April 9, 1865.

GEN. R. E. LEE,
　Commanding C. S. Army.

GENERAL,

Your note of yesterday is received.

As I have no authority to treat on the subject of peace, the meeting proposed for at 10 a.m. to-day could lead to no good. I will state, however, General, that I am equally anxious for peace, and the whole North entertain the same feeling. The terms upon which peace can be had are well understood.

By the South laying down their arms they will hasten that most desirable event, save thousands of lives, and hundreds of millions of property not yet destroyed.

Hoping that all our difficulties may be settled without the loss of another life,

I remain,
Your obd'nt Servant,
U. S. GRANT, Lt.-General,
Commanding U. S. Army.

April 9, 1865.

GENERAL,

I received your note of this morning, on the picket line, where I had come to meet you, and ascertain definitely what terms were embraced in your proposition of yesterday, with reference to the surrender of this army.

I now request an interview, in accordance with the offer contained in your letter of yesterday, for that purpose.

Your obd'nt Servant,
R. E. LEE, General.

LT.-GEN. GRANT,
Commanding U. S. Army.

April 9, 1865.

Gen. R. E. Lee,
Commanding C. S. Army.

General,

Your note of this date is but this moment (11.50 a.m) received.

In consequence of having passed from the Richmond and Lynchburg road, I am at this moment writing about four miles west of Walters' Church, and will push forward to the front for the purpose of meeting you.

Notice sent to me on this road where you wish the interview to take place, will meet me.

Very respectfully,
U. S. Grant,
Lt.-General.

Appomattox Court House,
April 9, 1865.

Gen. R. E. Lee,
Commanding C. S. Army:

General,—In accordance with the substance of my letter to you of the 8th instant, I propose to receive the surrender of the army of Northern Virginia on the following terms, to wit:

Rolls of all the officers and men to be made in duplicate, one copy to be given to an officer designated by me, the other to be retained by such officer as you may designate.

The officers to give their individual parole not to take arms against the government of the United States until properly exchanged, each company or regimental commander to sign a parole for the men of their commands.

The arms, artillery and public property to be parked and stacked, and turned over to the officers appointed by me to receive them. This will not embrace the side arms of the officers, nor their private horses or baggage.

This done, each officer and man will be allowed to return to their homes, not to be disturbed by the United States authorities so long as they shall observe their parole and the laws in force where they may reside.

Very respectfully,
U. S. GRANT, Lt.-Gen.

Head-Quarters Army Northern Virginia, April 9, 1865.

Lt.-Gen. U. S. Grant,
  Commanding U. S. Army:

General,—I have received your letter of this date, containing the terms of the surrender of the army of Northern Virginia, as proposed by you. As they are substantially the same as those expressed in your letter of the 8th instant, they are accepted. I will proceed to designate the proper officers to carry the stipulations into effect.

Your obd't serv't,
R. E. LEE, General.

THE MEETING.

Generals Lee and Grant met at the house of Mr. Wilmer McLean. General Lee was attended only by Colonel Marshal, one of his aids. As to Grant he had several officers with him. The two commanders greeted each other with courtesy.

General Lee at once alluded to the conditions of the surrender, and said he would leave the details to Gen. Grant's discretion. The latter stated the terms of the parole, namely: that the arms should be stacked, the artillery parked, and the supplies and munitions turned over to him, the officers to retain their side arms, horses and personal effects. To these terms General Lee promptly agreed, and the agreement was engrossed, and signed by General Lee at half-past three p. m.

During this meeting a strange scene was taking place between the lines of the two armies. The streets of the village of Appomattox were filled with groups of officers of both sides. On the United States side were to be seen Generals Sheridan, Ord, Crook, Gibbon, Merritt and others; while on the other side there were Generals Longstreet, Gordon, Heth, Wilcox and some other officers.

This mingling of late foes lasted about one hour and a half. Only general officers were allowed to pass the picket line. At first these gallant men only took distant looks at each other; then they mingled, and hands were shaken, and the reserve began to wear off. Some one produced the *aqua vitæ* of the soldier—whisky,—and healths were drunk. By degrees, the area of this meeting widened; and, before it was over, the groups of men had grown so social, that some were to be seen seated on the steps of the houses, while others took their seats on a fence.

Between the lines of the two armies there was great suspense. The two skirmish lines stood man to man before each other, and all were eager to hear if peace was made. The line of the Confederate army skirted a strip of woods in rear of the town, and glimpses of it could be caught through the vistas of the streets.

The minutes passed slowly. An eager look was cast at every horseman who came on the ground. Two P.M. was the time appointed by General Grant for the resumption of hostilities. It came, and the skirmish line of the United States army began to advance. A moment more, and the crack of the rifle would have ushered in the work of death; but a clatter of hoofs was heard, and a flag of truce came upon the ground, with an order from General Grant to cease hostilities until further orders,—and the men lay at a rest.

After the interview at McLean's house, General Lee returned to his camp, about half a mile distant, where his leading officers were awaiting his return. He announced the result, and the terms. They then went up to him, in the order of their rank, and shook hands, expressing their satisfaction at his course and their regret at parting, all shedding tears on the occasion.

The fact of surrender and the forms were then announced to the troops, and, when General Lee appeared among them, he was loudly cheered.

E

FINALE,—APRIL 11.

Headquarters, Army of the Potomac,
Farmville, April 11, 1865.

The last vestige of the Army of Northern Virginia being now broken up, the Army of the Potomac seems at a loss to know what to do or where to go.

PAROLING THE ENEMY.

All day yesterday was employed in carrying out the terms of surrender and paroling the prisoners. Contrary to the expectation and wish of a large portion of the army, there was no public or formal surrender in the presence of our army; but it was conducted quietly by Generals Grant and Lee. This was, I learn, in accordance with the wish of both these generals.

The men are not to be paroled individually, but each company officer makes himself responsible for his men, colonels for their regiments, brigade commanders for their brigades, division commanders for their divisions, and General Lee for the whole. The number now present for parole is very small, a large portion of the army having scattered to their respective homes after they were surrendered. Gen. Rosser with 600 cavalry has gone off, and it is not known where he now is.

THE TWO ARMIES KEPT APART.

Very little communication was allowed between the two armies, none but officers having special permission being permitted to visit them.

The large mass of the private soldiers seem perfectly content with the arrangement, their only solicitation being for the welfare of General Lee, for whom they entertain the strongest affection. When assured no harm would be done him they were glad the thing was over.

FEELING OF THE SOLDIERY TOWARD DAVIS.

For Davis they entertain anything but feelings of love, and many expressed the wish that we might catch him and hang him. They said if they caught him they would save us the trouble.

VISIT TO GENERAL LEE.

General Meade, accompanied by Generals Webb, Hunt and others of his staff, visited General Lee yesterday. Their interview was short but agreeable. General Lee is very reserved in his manner, but extremely polite and courteous. His headquarters consisted of a fly drawn over a pole, while his staff were sitting about on logs before small fires. Many of his staff and other officers displayed bad taste in indulging in their usual game of brag.

It was the wish of our officers to drop all subjects of conversation which would be unpleasant to them, but they would constantly recur to battles in which they claim to have defeated us, and of their ability to do so again. Many of our officers came back disgusted.

DISPERSION OF THE ARMY.—APRIL 23.

Hdqrs. Army of the Potomac,
April 23, 1865.

This army is now being broken up. The Sixth Corps, which has earned the word *Ubique*, and might bear it on its flag, was put in march this morning for Danville, in order to hold that point, and, it would seem, to guard the communications of the army under Gen. Sherman.

The Fifth Corps is now posted along the Southside Railroad, guarding that line, and the Ninth, which did that duty till lately, is now on its way to the Capital, from which, report says, it will be transported to a certain distant point of the Confederate country.

The Twenty-fourth Corps is in march for Richmond, where the bulk of it now is; and lastly the Second Corps is here waiting for orders.

THE DANVILLE RAILROAD.

The President of this Road was at these headquarters up to yesterday, and made an offer to put the line in running order on certain terms. These terms were not accepted at first, but afterward Gen. Grant directed the General commanding to accept the offer if the party took the oath of allegiance. This has not been done, and yesterday the President left.

Now that the Sixth Corps is to operate by this line of road it is necessary to have it in running order; and it is to be expected that the directory will comply with the conditions mentioned by Gen. Grant.

OUR COMMUNICATIONS.

are good, though the track of the S. S. R. R. is still so uneven and the rail so worn that trains cannot run faster than about six miles an hour. Men are at work on the track, and each day new ties are laid and loose rails made firm, so that the track is at least safe now.

The foot roads are in good order, thanks to the dry weather, and the army wants nothing but a season of rest and recreation, and then it will want—time will show what.

The Cavalry and the Sixth Corps were sent toward Danville; and the other Corps lay at a rest about Burkesville for some days. This ended the campaign.

THE DEFENSE OF THE PROVINCES.

CANADA.

The Provinces being at this time menaced with a raid or attack, a few notes on general defense will be timely.

The first thing to do in placing a country in a state of defense, is to divide it into sections, according to its extent. Now, the extent of Canada is very great, and the country ought to be divided into three sections, to be termed Districts.

These Districts would form the East, Centre and West of Canada, and would be designated the 1st, 2nd and 3rd Districts,—or the Eastern, Centre, and Western.

In each District, then, there would be a Staff appointed to organize the force there, by directions from an Adjutant-General, and a point would be designated as District Headquarters. The force so organized would form a Corps of the general forces of the province.

At the Capital (Ottawa) would be General Headquarters, from which orders would be issued to District Headquarters, and the prompt action in time of war, of the whole force be secured for the defense of any one point of the province.

ORGANIZATION.

The next thing to do is to organize the fighting men of the country; and, first, to estimate the number wanted for any emergency, so that an unnecessary force might not be called out. Now, 150,000 men, with what force Britain could send us, would be adequate to defend Canada. To form this force, only the young men would be required, and the ages for service might be from 18 to 35 only. A second class of men might be reserved to fill up the battalions, in time of war.

GENERAL STAFF.

This might consist of an Adjutant-General and an Assistant, with a few other officers, all to be selected for their talent. The capital would, in time of peace, be general headquarters.

DISTRICT STAFFS.

These would consist of two A. A. Generals, the inferior to act as Assistant and Inspector for the force in the District. Certain points would be designated as their headquarters.

FIRST DISTRICT.

In order that there might be as little change in the present system of organization as possible, battalions should be formed as they are now, except that they should consist of about 650 men, in six companies. This is the proper strength for militia, if everything is considered. It would be well also if there were a second " guide " to each company, (the covering sergeant being one) for it would render action more easy and correct.

Numbers ought then to be given to regiments. This is all the change I would advise for the present.

The A. A. General of the District would organize the force into brigades and divisions. Though the Corps could be fully organized and enrolled, only a part could be called out for drill a number of days in the year, and this part ought to be the staffs of battalions, each of which would form a provisional company.

The question then would be what to do with the present " Active Militia." To avoid change, it might remain as it is, the battalions in each new district to form so many of the corps of that district; but what I have said about " guides " ought to be adopted in this force.

The limits of the 1st District might be from the Gulf to Three Rivers, inclusive. Headquarters to be at Quebec.

SECOND DISTRICT.

In this District, which would be the most important one, the organization would, of course, be the same as in the first. I would only say that, west of the 1st District, the forces ought to be kept in a more ready state than in the east, the line of frontier being more open to the attacks of an enemy.

The limits of the 2nd District might be from Three Rivers to the foot of Lake Ontario. Headquarters to be at Montreal.

THIRD DISTRICT.

In regard to attacks, this District would be the most exposed, and it would also be the farthest from

Canada's base of supply. The force organized in it, could not be too well cared for, or be held in too ready a state, in a time like the present.

The limits of the 3rd District might be from the foot of Lake Ontario to the western boundary line. Headquarters to be at Toronto.

By this plan of organization, the forces of Canada would be in as ready a state for action as economy would allow. *Every man would know his place, and every officer his command.* As little as possible would be left to be done in an emergency, for then there is no time for anything to be done well.

THE REFORM

required by this plan, in the present system, would be slight. In the first place, it would be easy to divide the country into three districts; then it would be equally easy to appoint District Staffs,—the present staffs might be used for the purpose; and lastly, the A. A. Generals of Districts could re-organize the battalions, and brigade and division them. The Active Militia would not undergo any change, for this is no time for it; but it would be under the orders of the same officer as the rest of the force of the District. There is nothing in this change to deter the Administration from making it.

THE PRESENT ENEMY.

The enemy who at this time break the peace are not so numerous as to excite any fears; but they are dangerous enough to oblige us to arm and have ready 30,000 men, including the regular force in Canada, which I estimate at 8,000 men, for duty.

The list of Fenian forces given by the N. Y. *World* is not correct, of course, for it is meant to "crack up" a bad cause. There can not be more than 30 to 35,000 men in course of organization by the Fenian leaders. The main points at which this is going on are Chicago, St. Louis, and New York, and there the best men are picked up. I mean best as to soldierly qualities. It is not likely that this force can be much increased before the Fenians strike, for they must do so soon; but it is possible that they may get 50,000 men under arms for the month of April.

QUALITY OF THE FENIAN FORCES.

The quality of the Fenian forces is not to be despised, for very many of the men—some thousands, have been in the late war, and these would not be unsteady under fire. Then the fighting spirit of the whole is good, for the men are of a fighting race.

Many of the officers are men of some ability, and few of them have not courage. In the late armies of the United States there were during the four years of war, about 400,000 Irish. One-fourth of them is gone, and another fourth is disabled, from wounds or broken health. Of the remaining half 100,000 might like another taste of war, while as many more have had enough of it. It is from the estimated 100,000 men, still for fight, that the Fenians get their best men; and they may have 15,-000 of this class. The rest of their force is made up of young fellows from 17 to 20 years of age, who were too young to take part in the late war, and men who did not go out.

POINTS OF ATTACK.

The line of frontier presents many points of attack. In the east, there is the line from Rouse's Point to St. Regis, etc. In the west there are the lines of the Niagara, Detroit and St. Clair rivers, and the frontier from Cornwall to above Prescott. All of these were tried by the United States forces in the war of 1812-'14, and there was no great difficulty about getting on the Canada side.

It is very likely that the Fenians would follow in the steps of the Enemy of that time; and I think that, from the Detroit to the St. Clair, is the line along which they will make efforts to pass the frontier. In the east they could be more readily met than in the far west, and, therefore, they will hardly try an inroad down there,—though it is easy enough to get "over the border" from Rouse's Point to St. Regis, there being no great obstructions. If they tried this, however, they would be met by all the regular troops at the posts of Montreal and Quebec, and the *élite* of the Volunteer Militia,—in all 20,000 men, better in most points than their best men.

It seems to be their intention to make their base in the West, and to try some points along the frontier up there for a crossing, then to hurry over at the successful point all their force, and so cast the die. If they, at the same time, make some feints at other points, they may get over, provided they can raise a greater force than that opposed to them.

DEFENSE.

It is not at all difficult for 35,000 men, with a chain of rivers and lakes covering a great part of the frontier, to drive back any bodies of Fenians that may cross the line; though it is possible that some body or bodies of them may gain a footing on Canadian soil. The cause in which the Canadian forces would fight is the best men could shed their blood for, and, therefore, they ought to fight in the very best spirit.

The points most to guard and hold are the lines of the Niagara and Detroit rivers; next to these, the frontier from Rouse's Point to St. Regis, and from Cornwall to above Prescott. A good force of Rifle Corps, with some guns on the river lines, ought to be thrown out upon the frontier, and, at the most convenient points in rear, the bulk of the forces of Canada should be concentrated. In the East, Montreal is the proper point in winter for reserves to the force on the frontier from Rouse's Point to St. Regis. In the Spring a part of the reserves might be encamped about St. Johns and St. Lambert. In that position they would be ready to cross to the north side of the St. Lawrence by the Bridge, or to move out by rail to the frontier.

In the West, St. Catharines and Hamilton are the points for reserves to the force posted along the Niagara. In the Spring the reserves might all be encamped about St. Catharines, it being nearer to the frontier. The reserves to the force posted along the Detroit and St. Clair rivers, would in winter lie about London, from which they could be sent either to Sarnia or to Windsor. In Spring a part might be thrown forward to within a few miles of the Detroit.

Of all these points that about Prescott is now the most important, for it is the outpost to the Capital, which is only 54 miles back of it. It would be well, therefore, to post in the Spring a strong reserve on the best point in rear of Prescott, and to have the line of the G. T. Railroad from that point to Cornwall well guarded, that this means to bring up troops from Montreal might not be broken, by a sudden dash of the enemy.

The next thing to care for would be a ready means of transport for men from one point of the country to another, and to this end the G. T. and G. W. Railroads ought to have trains and engines reserved for the carriage of 2,000 men each, at a time. By crowding the men on top of the cars as well as inside, as I have seen done in the late war, a large force could be very soon carried to any point attacked. The line of the Grand Trunk is liable to be cut, and there are no good back roads, so that these would be disadvantages with which we would have to contend, but, with the present enemy, there is nothing to fear.

The force that it would be well to post at the various points, and those points, are as follows:—

At Montreal,	5,000	men.
Back of Prescott,	5,000	"
From St. Regis to the Richelieu,	3,000	"
At other posts in the East,	2,000	"
At St. Catharines,	5,000	"
At London,	5,000	"

On the lines of the Niagara,
Detroit and St. Clair rivers, 5,000 "
At other posts in the West, - 5,000 "

Total, - - - - 35,000

This for the spring. In the winter months (if it be found necessary to continue in a state of defense) the forces would of course be drawn back for winter quarters.

All the regular force in the East ought to be gathered about Montreal and Prescott; all in the West, about St. Catharines and London.

THE UNITED STATES AS THE ENEMY.

If it were a war with the United States instead of with the Fenians, our task would be far less easy, and there would be reason for some fears. Instead of 35,000 men, 150,000 would be wanted; and even then Canada might be overrun by the enemy, who could send 200 or 250,000 men over the frontier, if necessary. So certain, however, are they of their ability to take Canada, that they would try it with 80 to 100,000 men; and in that confidence would lie our safety, for we could meet them with something like an equality of force.

PLAN OF CAMPAIGN.

There are many ways in which to attack Canada, and it is likely that the plan of campaign of the American general would be to strike a vital blow by the shortest line of advance. My idea is, that he would make a feint at the Niagara, and throw three corps of his army across the St. Lawrence at points from Cornwall to Prescott. One of these corps he would at once march to the Ottawa, and with the other two he could turn west and overrun the country. In doing this, he would despatch a division to take the Capital, and hold it,—and to act as a reserve to the corps on the Ottawa. This body would take position on the river, and isolate the West from the East.

In the meantime, if the force in front of the first corps were withdrawn, or lessened, that body would convert its feint into a real attack, pass the Niagara and move upon Hamilton, there seize the depot of the G. W. Railroad, and, leaving a force at the point, march east to meet the column coming west. In this way a vital blow *might* be struck,—the west overrun, and the Capital taken. Of course it is easier to say than to do, and things *might* turn up to foil the plan; but that the plan is feasible, I know very well.

A SECOND PLAN

might be to make a point in the west a base, and to march east, fighting the way to the Ottawa river. To do this, a corps would make a feint in the east, say at Rouse's Point, and three corps would pass the Niagara and march upon Hamilton, in the vicinity of which a battle would be fought. After this the Enemy would march east.

In the meantime, if the force in front of the first corps were withdrawn, it would push into Canada, and, reaching the St. Lawrence, would pass, or feign to pass, the river, which would keep a large force in observation on the other side of it.

If the Enemy gained the line of the Ottawa, they would cross that shallow stream, by pontoons or other means, and march upon Montreal. It is likely that a battle would be fought on the head of the Island of Montreal, for the city. If the Canadian forces were hard pressed, and the body covering the city were withdrawn, the first corps would cross the river and endeavor to take in rear the forces fighting on the island.

This plan is also feasible, and, though the Island

of Montreal might not be taken, Canada West would have to go, unless an equal force could be pitted against the enemy. The command of Lake Ontario would, of course, very much influence the result of the contest.

A THIRD PLAN

might be to take and hold Canada south of the St. Lawrence. It would be easy to do this, for there are no 'great obstructions to the advance of an enemy. That section *would have to go.* The gain by the acquisition of this strip of territory would be the navigation of the St. Lawrence to the Gulf.

HOW TO MEET THIS.

To meet all this a force of 150,000 men would be necessary, of which 30,000 ought to be British. This seems a very large force, but it is small, considering the extent of the frontier. These 150,000 men, in four corps, would have to be placed as follows :—

East.

About Montreal and St. Lambert, one corps, in reserve, 30,000 men.

From Island Pond to the head of the Richelieu, and thence to St. Regis, one corps, - - 30,000 "

West.

From Cornwall to Toronto, with one division of the reserve, back of Prescott, one corps, - - - - - - - - 30,000 "

F

From Toronto to the Niagara, Detroit and St. Clair rivers, with a reserve at Hamilton and a second at London, one corps, - - - - - - - -   40,000 men.
                                                          ─────────
                                                          130,000 "
Cavalry and Artillery, - - -   10,000 "
Separate division along the Maine frontier, communicating with New Brunswick, -   10,000 "
                                                          ─────────
Total, - - - - -   150,000 "

This would be, for Canada, an immense host; but, scattered over its vast territory, it would by no means crowd the country. Except about Montreal, there would not be any great mass of men. Not *one* man of this force could Canada spare in a war, if the United States were to put forth their full strength, or half of it, for its conquest.

In the face of this I think it is possible, *with men of talent at our head*, and all the aid, naval and land, that Britain could send us, to defend Canada, or the best part of it.

OUR STRATEGY.

In the first place, the link between the two sections of Canada should be held at any cost, that the enemy might not isolate the West from the East, and take the Capital, though, in a strategical point of view, Ottawa is not of much consequence. Holding Central Canada, we could regain the West, if it were at first lost.

Then it would be well to hold one corps well in

hand, to be thrown to any point attacked; and this corps ought, as I have shown, to be about Montreal, on both sides of the river. From this point it could be moved out to reinforce the corps on the eastern frontier, or be sent up to the line from Cornwall to Prescott. All, or nearly all, of the regular force in Canada ought to be in this body, for it should be the *elite* of the army—the Xth legion of it.

On the line of the Ottawa there ought to be a chain of works, including some *tetes des ponts*, to enable a force to hold the right bank, for it must be expected that the enemy might get into Central Canada, and reach the river.

On the south side of the St. Lawrence there ought also to be a line of works, which could be readily connected by rifle pits, enclosing the village of St. Lambert. This to be one and a-half to two miles from the bank of the river, (for the enemy would have to be kept at such a distance from Montreal, that they could not bombard it), and, of course, to cover Montreal and the Victoria Bridge. It would not be necessary to have continuous works, but only detached ones, which could be connected on any front by rifle pits.

I will now show in what way the two principal plans of attack of the enemy could be met, and first as to that on Central Canada.

ATTACK ON CENTRAL CANADA.

This would be made at some point from Cornwall to Prescott. At the very first development of the plan, the corps in Central Canada would concentrate at the point of attack, and the reserves about Montreal would be put in march to the same point. The first corps could hold the enemy in check for some time. If it could do so until the arrival of the reserves from Montreal, the enemy would be foiled in their attempt to gain a footing on the left bank of the river at that point; but, if it could not, the two corps ought to give battle as soon as the second had come up, before the enemy had all their force over the river.

In the meantime the commanding general ought to telegraph for the nearest division of the two corps in the East and West, and these would come, as far as possible, by rail.

If the battle were won, the enemy would be thrown back upon the river, and be driven across it with great loss. Their crossings would be pontoon bridges, and these would also be lost to them. If, on the contrary, the two corps were defeated, they ought to fall back, with their right covering the road to the Capital, and their left moving toward the Ottawa. As they did so, they would dispute all the ground to gain time for reinforcements to get up. The new line would extend obliquely from the direction of the capital to the St. Lawrence, the left touching the river. With a line of such an extent, it would not be safe to enter into any serious fight with the enemy; and our object ought to be only to check them, and defend certain points as far as it could be done.

After the defeat of the two corps, the enemy might move upon Ottawa or Montreal, or upon both. It is likely that they would send a column to Ottawa, and march the mass of their forces to the Ottawa river. In that case the right of our forces would defend the capital, (which ought to be covered by works,) while the rest concentrated on the left, the two bodies to be connected by cavalry.

A second battle would then be fought on the right bank of the Ottawa, and the enemy would be checked, if not arrested in their advance, for by this time the force in the east telegraphed for would have come up, and our army would fight appuied on the works there thrown up. It would hold the right bank in spite of all the efforts of the enemy, if well handled.

Pending this, the force in the West telegraphed for would come up, and ought then to attack their communication at the point of crossing on the St. Lawrence. By this combination the enemy might be forced to fall back to that point, and get over the river in the best way they could.

ATTACK UPON THE WEST.

The second, if not the first, plan of the enemy would be to attack the West at points on the Niagara and Detroit rivers, as they did in 1812-'14.

It is likely that a corps would make a feint in the east to divert attention from the real point of attack, and that two corps would pass the Niagara, while one more would cross the Detroit. To meet this, as soon as the plan was developed, our corps in the west would concentrate at the two points, while that in Central Canada would move west, and the reserves about Montreal would move up to take up its line of defense. By this movement two corps would be concentrated to meet the attack, and, if necessary, a part of the reserve corps could be also sent to the point in danger.

If the enemy carried their corps in the east up to the points of attack, in order to support the forces there, the mass of our corps in its front could also be moved west, by which there would be a corresponding increase of force there in our army.

In case of success on our part, the enemy would be forced back upon the two rivers, and would lose heavily in material as well as men. If, on the contrary, they met with success, their columns would march upon Hamilton and Toronto, partly by the lines of the G. W. and G. T. Railroads. At the latter city the enemy would unite, and it is likely that about there would be fought a second battle for its possession. Again, if—for there must be many " ifs " in these operations,—the enemy got the best of us there also, they would march east, fighting their way to the Ottawa river. At this part of the campaign a reserve corps might be crossed from Ogdensburg, to meet the main body, or to take in rear our retreating forces.

On our part, as soon as it would be seen that our force in the West was over-matched, all the reserve corps sent to Central Canada ought to be pushed west, while the corps in the east, leaving only a strong line of pickets and a few small reserves there, would move into Central Canada, to take the place of the latter. In this way all our forces would be thrown in the path of the enemy, and their progress be arrested. If they, in this case, tried to pass a corps over the St. Lawrence, at or near Ogdensburg, our corps from the east would meet the attempt and foil it.

The field of battle would then be Western Canada, the enemy in the west of it, our forces in the east; and, until our forces could be augmented in some way, the enemy would hold the Peninsula. Here I may observe that the longer they would be allowed to stay there, the more difficult it would be to drive them out of it. Let it be imagined, however, that, finally, they would be driven over the frontier. This I could only hope, if they got so far into Canada.

From this it will be seen that success on our part would depend upon striking the enemy with full force before they would get all their corps over the chain of rivers, and united at certain points.

As to the third plan of the enemy,—that is, to take Canada south of the St. Lawrence,—they would go about it by making a feint on the west, say at Niagara, and then pouring the bulk of their forces over the line by way of Plattsburg, Rouse's Point and Island Pond, using the lines of railroad leading to those places, to bring up supplies.

To meet this three of our corps could concentrate on that strip of territory, while the fourth, in the west, would extend to the east, and take up the position left by the corps of Central Canada. So easy would it be, however, for the enemy to get all their forces on our soil at this point, that the chances are they could take and hold that part of our territory.

Such is a brief consideration of the attack and defense of Canada.

NEW BRUNSWICK.

This Province has a much shorter line of frontier to defend than Canada, but, at the same time, it has a much smaller number of fighting men. It has the advantage of some small seaports, to which forces could be sent during the winter.

THE LINE

runs from St. Andrews to the River St. Francis, and most of it runs through interminable woods.

It would be easy for an enemy to pass this line at many points, for there are no obstructions of any consequence about it. The St. Croix River runs along the line for some distance into the interior, but this would not retard an enemy for any time, if well provided with pontoon trains.

THE CAPITAL,

Fredericton, lies on the St. John River, at no great distance from the frontier, and well open to attack. It is, however, of easy access from St. John, the principal seaport, lying at the mouth of the river. This would, in a war, be the base of supply to the Province. Shediac would also be a point for supplies, which could be readily carried to St. John, and thence to the Capital or other interior points, there being a short line of railroad between the two first places.

THE PRESENT ENEMY.

If the Fenians decide to attack New Brunswick, they could throw 25,000 to 30,000 men against it. They could not gather as many men in the State of Maine for the attack, or raid, as they would be able to do along the frontier of Canada; but this they would not need to do; and, besides, the points to attack being fewer than in the other province, they could act in more concentrated form. As to the quality of this enemy, it has been referred to in the article on Canada, so that it need not be now gone over. I will only say that they ought not to be despised.

POINTS OF ATTACK.

There are two points on the frontier that would likely be selected for attack, and they are St. Stephen and St. Andrews. They are near each other, and from one runs a road to the Capital,—from the other a road to St. John. A naval force could very much assist in the defence of St. Andrews, which is on a tongue of land, and, therefore, a naval force would be wanted by the enemy to take it.

These two points might be simultaneously attacked, and on their being taken, the enemy might march in two columns upon the Capital and St. John. These two places in their hands, the west of the province would be lost—at least for a time—to its people.

From St. John the enemy would then march, by the line of railroad, to Shediac, and take the other places lying in the North and East. All this would take time, and I only mention these operations as possible to an active and well-led enemy.

It would be very difficult for the enemy to take St. John, if it were aided by a strong naval force; and it would be, of course. To get on the left bank of the river, the enemy would have to cross some miles up it, and would be more or less checked by the fire of light gun-boats. It is very possible that St. John could be held in spite of all the efforts of an enemy like the present one; and it would require a strong force of U. S. troops and a large number of iron-clads to take the point in the face of the naval force that Britain could send there.

TO MEET THIS,

it would be necessary to have at least 25,000 men in the province, of whom 6 to 8,000 ought to be regular troops. A good militia force of 15 to 20,000 men could be formed in the province, and this, with the regular force, would be adequate to repel the attacks of the present enemy; but all the force that New Brunswick could raise, with all that Britain could send it, would not be enough to save the country, if the United States were the enemy. The force estimated for defence—25,000 men—might be placed as follows:—

At St. John - - - -	5,000 men.
At St. Andrews - - -	5,000 "
About St. Stephen - -	10,000 "
From that point, North along the frontier -	5,000 ".
Total - - -	25,000 "

No force need be placed at the Capital, for it would be covered by this disposition. In winter it would, of course, be necessary to withdraw some of the forces at the front to points in rear, for better quarters, and then 5 to 6,000 might be placed about Fredericton; but the mass of the army could winter on the frontier in log-huts, to build which there would be plenty of timber, for New Brunswick is a land of wood, and with good fires, the troops could pass the winter in tolerable comfort, as the forces on both sides, in the late war in the United States, did for four years.

ATTACK BY WAY OF ST. STEPHEN.

If the enemy made their attack by way of St. Stephen, which is the likely point, the 20,000 men placed along the frontier from St. Andrews to the North, would concentrate about the point and meet the attack. At the same time the division at St. John would be sent to the support of the rest of the force, and a battle would be fought.

If this were won by the Provincial forces, the enemy would be driven over the line, and the campaign would be over, with very little damage to the country. If, on the contrary, they lost the battle, the forces would have to fall back in two columns upon the capital and St. John, the mass of the army going toward the former place.

As soon as this result became known, all the disposable men in the country, from Shediac and other points, ought to concentrate about Fredericton. If the enemy did not send a column to St. John, the force intended for the defense of that place might also go to the capital. It is likely, however, that they would march upon both places if they met with success on the frontier. Some 30 to 40,000 men could in this way be gathered about the Capital, and a second battle would be fought for the point. Here, if the enemy could not present an equal force, they might be defeated, and driven back to the frontier, or to any position they might have fortified, to be prepared for a reverse. From this they might, in time, be forced by a combined effort of all the forces.

Should the capital also fall into the hands of the enemy, the Provincial forces might fall back behind the river St. John, and oppose its passage by their antagonists. Here again a sharp fight would take place, and it is possible the enemy could get no further. If, however, they could cross the river, the Provincial forces would fall back into the east of the country toward Shediac, which would be the new base, communication with St. John being kept up. In the East the contest might be prolonged for some time.

As to St. John, it could be put into such a state of defense by a division of the forces, aided by a naval force, that the enemy could do no more than shut up the body there, and keep it from the field. There would be a sharp fight for the E. & N. A. Railroad to Shediac, a short line, but one of importance. If the force of the enemy operating in this part of the province were greater than that defending St. John, it might leave a division before the city, and march east along the line of railroad to Shediac, while the main column moved upon the capital, and, if successful, beyond it.

On the other hand, if the corps of the enemy before St. John were repulsed, the provincial force there could send a part up the river to the capital to reinforce the army there. Again, if the main body covering the capital met with early success, it could send a part to reinforce the force about St. John, and in the end the enemy might be driven over the frontier. If the contest were to be carried over the country in this way, however, the damage done would be very great.

ATTACK BY WAY OF POINTS NORTH OF ST. STEPHEN

North of St. Stephen an enemy could pass the frontier at several points, and this would be the easier way; but, if the object were to attack St. John, this line of advance would be too indirect. For an attack upon the Capital, it would do very well, though the best roads leading to the place run from St. Stephen.

If the plan of the enemy were to move upon Fredericton, take it, and then to march in two columns upon St. John and Shediac, the first column going down the St. John river,—the line of advance by points north of St. Stephen would be direct enough.

To meet this movement, all the forces on the frontier to the south of St. Stephen would concentrate upon it, and extend to the north. At the same time the division at St. John would move up the river to the capital, and thence advance to the front, acting in reserve to the rest of the forces gathered to meet the enemy.

If the capital fell into the hands of the enemy, the provincial forces would fall back, east, before them, sending a division to St. John for its defense, and then would take place a contest in the east for the country there. In any case it would be some time before the north of New Brunswick would fall into the hands of an invading force.

AID FROM CANADA.

The next thing to consider is the aid that Canada might be free to send to the sister province in the event of the latter only being invaded.

There is a force of at least 8,000 regulars now in Canada, and 5,000 of them might be sent to the other province to reinforce the troops there. By holding the remaining 3,000 in Central Canada, with the bulk of them at Montreal, all would be quite safe against an enemy like the Fenian one.

A road runs from Riviere du Loup in Canada to St. Stephen, and this can be used for sending troops to New Brunswick at all seasons of the year, while they can also be sent, as long as navigation is open, from Quebec to Shediac. From this point they would be sent by rail to St. John, and thence to the capital. If the enemy got the best of the force in New Brunswick at first, this force from Canada would arrive in time to change the fortune of the war.

If Canada were the object of attack, any spare regular troops in New Brunswick could in the same way be sent to it. The force would not be of much weight in the contest there, for it would number only some 1500 men. In the absence of this small regular force, the militia of the Province would be able

to hold the important points. In this interchange
of aid the Intercolonial railroad would be of great
use, the more so in winter. It is New Brunswick
that would derive the most benefit from the road, as
it would more need aid from Canada than the latter
from it. The line of the road would be liable to be
cut by the enemy, as it would run so close to the
frontier in the north.

THE UNITED STATES AS THE ENEMY.

In this case, as in that of Canada, it would be very
difficult to defend New Brunswick. In fact, I do not
think it could be defended, though St. John might be
defended by means of a heavy naval force of iron-
clads. So open is the frontier to attack, that a force
of 100,000 men could be passed over it readily, and
before this, with any reserves that the enemy might
see fit to send after the other corps, point after point
would have to fall, in spite of our best efforts. It is
true, that 80,000 to 100,000 men might be gathered
for the defence of the province, but the enemy could
always have 50,000 more than we, by adding to their
army as we might do to our forces.

PLAN OF CAMPAIGN.

There are two plans which the enemy might adopt.
One would be to attack New Brunswick by way of
St. Stephen and points north of it, and to march upon
the capital and St. John; the other might be to pass
the frontier at St. Andrews and St. Stephen, a naval
force co-operating with the column at the first place,

and to march simultaneously upon St. John and the capital, a force of iron-clads to attack the first place at the same time. Unless the U. S. naval force were stronger than ours in the Bay of Fundy, however, the second plan could not be carried out.

The first plan of campaign, then, is the only one which I will point out. Entering the province from St. Stephen and points north of it, the U. S. forces would march upon the capital, and on the way would have to fight a battle for it. This, it is to be thought, they would win, and, as a consequence, the capital would change hands. From the capital they would march in two columns upon St. John and Shediac, for both of which points they would again have to fight. Success on their part would, I think, be the result, and the east and north of the country would in time fall into their hands. In the north the war might linger for some time, as, up there, the thick woods would afford cover for irregular warfare, and the Miramichi River would be a new point for supply.

If the enemy followed the force in the north-west by the road to Riviere du Loup, they would enter Canada East, and reach the St. Lawrence.

Into the North the remains of the New Brunswick forces would have to retreat, except the division thrown into St. John, which would have to share the fate of the place. If driven from the soil, they would enter Canada, and there find rest and supplies. The latter would be sent to Riviere du Loup, which, for a time, would be a base. In this way the army of defence would have to effect three changes of base, namely, from St John to Shediac, Shediac to Miramichi, and from this place to Riviere du Loup.

This result could only be gained by hard fighting on the part of the U. S. army, and by an overpowering force, for, certainly, they would meet with strenuous resistance from the militia, fighting for hearths and homes, as well as from the regular troops, with their prestige and honor to preserve.

The length of the war would likely be only twelve months from the time of crossing the frontier, but in that short time the enemy would lose 30,000 to 40,000 men, and our loss would not be less than 20,000.

THE DEFENCE.

The force necessary to defend New Brunswick against this enemy would be 80,000 to 100,000 men, an deven then, I think the result would be defeat, for the reasons given. The army ought to be placed as follows :—

About the Capital, in reserve 25,000 men.
About St. Stephen and points
 North - - - - - - - 35,000 "
About St. John - - - - - 10,000 "
About St. Andrews - - - 10,000 "

 Total - - - - 80,000 "

As soon as the plan of the enemy showed itself, the forces on the frontier would concentrate on their right, and the reserves would move to the front. This would throw 70,000 men in the way of the enemy, and leave 10,000 at St. John, to meet any attack upon it.

A naval force, in which there ought to be half a

G

dozen good iron-clads, would then be posted to aid in the defence of St. John and St. Andrews. If some gun-boats could ascend the St. John River, they would command the stream, and aid in the defence of the capital.

About the capital and St. John there ought to be a chain of works, and at points along the frontier also there would be some earth-works thrown up.

If the first battle were lost, the provincial forces would fall back upon the capital, and the bulk of the division at St. John would be sent up the river to reinforce the army. Before the capital, then, a second fight would take place, with a better chance of success, for the works about there thrown up would *appui* the line of battle. If the enemy were again too strong, the forces would fall back to the other side of the river, and there make another stand. For some time they could dispute the passage of the river, and if at last forced back, they could retreat towards Shediac.

A corps ought, at this time, to be sent down the river, to defend St. John and the line of railroad to Shediac. The rest of the forces would fight for every mile of ground in the East, as they fell back. Pending this, an irregular force might be gathered in the North, which could fall upon the line of communication of the enemy as soon as it should grow so long as to offer points for attack. This would oblige the enemy to keep a large force on that line, and would check them, in some degree, in their advance.

On reaching the capital, the enemy would, as I have shown, send a column down the St. John River to attack the city, while the main body would push on to the East, following our forces in their retreat. A hard fight would then take place for St. John, and, with the aid of a strong naval force, it might hold out for some time. During this, the enemy would get round upon the E. & N. A. Railroad, and take the line as far as Shediac. Cut off, in this way, from aid from the interior, St. John would in time fall. In this case, the force there posted might be taken off by the naval force aiding in the defence of the point. The body of men thus saved could be carried round to Shediac, or, if it were in the hands of the enemy, to posts to the North of it—if necessary, to the Miramichi River, or to any point from which a junction could be made with the main body of the forces.

On the line of that river a vigorous defence might be made for some time, the left of the line resting near the mouth of it, and the right on the woods about its source. Here a rally for the defence of New Brunswick could be made, all the forces driven from the West and East, gathering up in the North.

If they were forced from that position, they might fall back towards Bathurst, and here again make a stand for some time, the little port serving as a new base of supply. If any reinforcements could be sent to the province at that crisis, they could be landed there easily enough.

By this time the enemy would have weakened their forces by posting bodies at the points gained, and keeping up communication between them. This would take 25,000 men from their force in the field, and their losses might be 25,000 more, so that they would move into the North with 50,000 men less than they did into the East. If, then, their original force was 100,000 or 125,000 men, it would be 50,000 or 75,000 for the final struggle up there.

On the other hand, if the provincial forces were at first 80,000 men, they would, when driven up into the North, number about 55,000 men, estimating the losses at 25,000. Now, if this were the result, the enemy could not go any farther until reinforcements came to them. Time would thus be gained for further defence, and the war would go; but, as the enemy could get all the reinforcements they might want, the final result would be in their favor.

A few words may now be said about the defense of Nova Scotia.

This province is so nearly isolated by sea, that it would be easy to defend it, for it is only by the isthmus connecting the province with the contiguous one, that any enemy could attack it by land. A good naval force, then, and a small land force would hold Nova Scotia against any enemy. The present one would not make any attempt to take it. It is only defense against the United States as the enemy that I will treat of in this short paper.

In the event of a war with the United States, the enemy would first take New Brunswick, and then march over the isthmus to attack Nova Scotia. This, then, would be the only point of attack by land. They might send a force of 50,000 men against the point, and, if successful, march by the line of railroad by way of Truro to Halifax. On the way they might detach a column to take Pictou, and this force would break off from the main body at the point of Truro.

If the enemy got as far as Halifax, they would then try to take this strong point; but, with all the advantages of the co-operation of a fine naval force in its defense, and communication with Britain, it might defy all their efforts. During this it would be necessary for them to send 25,000 men more into the country, in order to keep open their line of communication, and held the other points of importance.

The end of this attempt at conquest might be that the north and west of the province would fall into the hands of the enemy, while Halifax and the most part of the east and south would be held by the provincial forces.

THE DEFENSE.

At first a force of 25,000 to 30,000 men would be necessary to defend the province, and should the enemy increase their forces to 75,000 men, all the available men left should be put under arms to make an effort to expel the invading force.

The 25,000 men formed for defense might be placed as follows:—

At Halifax,	5,000 men.
On the Isthmus,	5,000 "
About Truro, (in reserve,)	10,000 "
At Windsor,	2,500 "
At Pictou,	2,500 "
Total,	25,000 "

By this disposition 5,000 men would be on the frontier, while 15,000 more lay in line from east to west in reserve, and holding the points of Pictou and

Windsor. The remaining 5,000 men would hold the important point of Halifax as the base of supply. In the east Pictou would also serve as a base of supply for that part of the province.

As soon as the enemy advanced against the Isthmus, the force at Truro would move to the frontier to support the division there. This would throw 15,000 men in the way of the enemy. At the same time 2,500 men might be sent north from Halifax, 1500 from Pictou, and as many more from Windsor. By this 5,500 men would be added to the force in the north, which would then number 20,500 men.

If the enemy forced their way over the isthmus, the remaining troops at Halifax, Pictou and Windsor could be sent north, while a new force might be raised to concentrate about those points.

A second stand could be made on the Cobequid Mountains, and there a fight would take place for the line of country from Truro to Pictou. If driven from there the force would fall back, halting in rear of the rivers to the south of it, and disputing every mile of ground. In this way, the army would, by operating on the line of railroad to Halifax, find itself in time back of that place. Appuied by the line of works that would be there thrown up, and with a strong naval force co-operating, the force could not be driven farther.

During this, all the forces that could be raised from a reserve class of men ought to gather about Windsor and Pictou, and attack the flanks of the enemy as they got more deeply into the interior. This would check their progress, and they might be confined to the Isthmus until a heavy reinforcement reached them, when they would again push on.

In this, as in the other invasions, numbers would decide the fate of the country. If the enemy did not send 50,000 more men against the province than it could raise, they would be unable to take the country, or, at least, to do more than take a few points on the frontier.

It would be easy to defend Prince Edward's Island, for only a nation that has command of the sea could attack it. With a small naval force stationed off some points on the coast, the island would be well enough cared for.

Such is a brief consideration of the attack and defense of the Maritime Provinces.

www.ingramcontent.com/pod-product-compliance
Lightning Source LLC
Chambersburg PA
CBHW031419160426
43196CB00008B/996